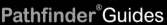
# Pathfinder®Guides

CU00950160

# The High Fells of Lakeland

Mountain Walks

*Written by*
*Terry Marsh*

# Contents

# At-a-glance

| Walk | Page | 🚩 | | 🏠 | 🚏 | ⛰ |
|------|------|-----|---|-----|-----|-----|
| **1** **High Pike and Carrock Fell** | 7 | Caldbeck Common | NY 354338 | 6¼ miles (10km) | 1,755ft (535m) |
| **2** **Skiddaw** | 10 | Underscar | NY 281253 | 10 miles (16km) | 2,855ft (870m) |
| **3** **Bowscale Fell, Bannerdale Crags and Souther Fell** | 14 | Mungrisdale | NY 364302 | 8 miles (12.7km) | 2,335ft (710m) |
| **4** **Blencathra: Sharp Edge and Scales Fell** | 18 | Scales | NY 343269 | 5¼ miles (8.5km) | 2,215ft (675m) |
| **5** **Blencathra: Hall's Fell Ridge and Doddick Fell** | 21 | Threlkeld | NY 324255 | 3¾ miles (6km) | 2,430ft (740m) |
| **6** **Causey Pike, Crag Hill and Grisedale Pike** | 24 | Stoneycroft | NY 233222 | 9¼ miles (15km) | 3,935ft (1,200m) |
| **7** **Hindscarth and Robinson** | 28 | Newlands valley (Rigg Beck) | NY 229201 | 7½ miles (12km) | 2,720ft (830m) |
| **8** **Grasmoor** | 31 | Rannerdale (Hause Point) | NY 163183 | 6¼ miles (10km) | 3,135ft (955m) |
| **9** **Red Pike, High Stile and High Crag** | 36 | Buttermere | NY 173169 | 7½ miles (12km) | 2,920ft (890m) |
| **10** **Pillar, Red Pike and Yewbarrow** | 39 | Wasdale (Overbeck Bridge) | NY 168068 | 10 miles (16km) | 4,725ft (1,440m) |
| **11** **Scafell Pike** | 42 | Seathwaite | NY 235122 | 8½ miles (13.5km) | 3,280ft (1,000m) |
| **12** **Great Gable** | 45 | Seathwaite | NY 235122 | 6¼ miles (10km) | 2,525ft (770m) |
| **13** **Base Brown, Green Gable, Brandreth and Grey Knotts** | 49 | Seatoller | NY 245138 | 8¾ miles (14km) | 2,790ft (850m) |
| **14** **Crinkle Crags and Bow Fell** | 55 | Langdale valley Old Dungeon Ghyll | NY 286061 | 9¼ miles (15km) | 3,610ft (1,100m) |
| **15** **Harrison Stickle and Pike of Stickle** | 59 | Great Langdale Old Dungeon Ghyll | NY 294064 | 6½ miles (10.5km) | 2,640ft (805m) |
| **16** **Old Man of Coniston and Dow Crag** | 62 | Coniston | SD 304975 | 8½ miles (13.5km) | 3,100ft (945m) |
| **17** **Wetherlam** | 66 | Tilberthwaite | NY 306010 | 5½ miles (8.75km) | 2,280ft (695m) |
| **18** **Great Dodd and Clough Head** | 71 | High Row, Matterdale | NY 380219 | 8 miles (13km) | 1,970ft (600m) |
| **19** **Sheffield Pike** | 74 | Glenridding | NY 386169 | 5 miles (8km) | 1,790ft (545m) |
| **20** **Helvellyn via Striding Edge and Grisedale** | 77 | Patterdale | NY 396159 | 10¾ miles (17.3km) | 3,605ft (1,100m) |
| **21** **Fairfield** | 81 | Ambleside | NY 377045 | 10½ miles (17km) | 3,525ft (1,075m) |
| **22** **St Sunday Crag** | 85 | Patterdale | NY 396159 | 8¾ miles (14km) | 2,755ft (840m) |
| **23** **Yoke, Ill Bell, Froswick and Thornthwaite Crag** | 88 | Troutbeck | NY 412027 | 11¼ miles (18.2km) | 3,150ft (960m) |
| **24** **High Street and Harter Fell** | 92 | Mardale Head | NY 469107 | 7 miles (11km) | 2,675ft (815m) |

## Walking safety

Wear appropriate footwear such as strong walking boots. Obtain local weather forecasts, and in the event of sudden bad weather, retreat by the safest possible route

# Comments

A visit to the grassy summit of Lakeland's most northerly fell, leading across breezy moorland to the vastly different summit of Carrock Fell, adorned with an Iron Age hill fort.

An energetic haul to the summit of one of Lakeland's most popular fells, concluding with an extended tour using an ancient trackway, now part of the Cumbria Way, across the moorlands Back o'Skidda'.

An easy ascent to Bowscale Fell, followed by a lovely romp across grassy upland before taking to the River Glenderamackin. The walk concludes with a trek across haunted Souther Fell.

Sharp Edge is a magnificent but woefully brief arête feeding into a little scrambling as you head for the top of the fell. The descent is long, straightforward and with spectacular views eastwards to the Pennines.

The most direct and shortest ascent to the top of Blencathra is followed by an equally delightful romp down neighbouring Doddick Fell. A little easy scrambling is needed at the top, but this is brief and can be avoided.

An excellent ridge of undulations links Causey Pike and Crag Hill; in between the two, Scar Crags and Sail provide ample opportunity to take in the stunning landscape of north-west Lakeland.

Two of Lakeland's most stunning fells linked in an elevated circuit of the delectable Newlands valley. Choose a fine day and dawdle, but *take care as you descend Robinson's north ridge.*

The distance is deceptive; with such height gain this is a major undertaking, but one that is massively worthwhile and enjoyable. Tackle the Rannerdale Knotts ridge at the end for an exquisite finish to the day.

This wall of rock on the south side of Buttermere involves a steep ascent, and a very steep descent on loose scree. *A great outing, but needing care and attention.*

A classic round of Lakeland fells that must be left for a fine day. The Pillar group of fells sit across the valley from England's highest, and provides an outstanding alternative to them.

This route is the finest to the summit of England's highest mountain and leads you through the very heart of Lakeland. Wait for a good walking day, when the tops are clear and the weather settled.

The icon of Lakeland, Great Gable is popular with walkers and rock climbers alike, and offers the most stunning view of Wasdale, and a chance to link the walk with neighbouring Green Gable.

A great circular tour of mountain upland at the head of Ennerdale concludes with a visit to a slate quarry and a steady descent from a high mountain pass.

After a gentle introduction, the walk rises sharply to gain the edge of rocky Crinkle Crags at the head of the Langdale valley. Here the walk is combined with adjacent Bow Fell, a shapely and popular fell.

The Langdale Pikes are arguably the most distinctive of Lakeland fell profiles; they attract thousands of visitors each year and hold a tantalising position above the valley, an attraction that few can resist.

The Old Man of Coniston has the distinction of being the first summit to which a 'tourist' ascent was made, in 1792. Today, it remains as popular as ever it was, dominating the village of Coniston.

This often-neglected summit lies above the hamlet of Tilberthwaite. Once popular with Victorian tourists who came to see the waterfalls, it remains as worthy an outing as any of the Coniston fells.

An outward walk along the length of the Dodds where you can visit the highest of these curvaceous fells is followed by a return along Old Coach Road, an ancient highway now used by ramblers and cyclists.

Glenridding is a launch pad for excursions to the summit of Helvellyn or Place Fell. Yet overlooking the village is shapely Sheffield Pike and Glenridding Dodd, offering excellent alternatives on busy days.

There is no finer way to a Lakeland summit than along Striding Edge, a narrow arête with significant drops on both sides. Here is an extended tour to visit Grisedale Tarn and the pleasures of the long Grisedale Valley.

Fairfield sits at the head of a ring of fells north of Ambleside. The complete circuit – known as the Fairfield Horseshoe – as described here is a major outing and is best reserved for a long summer's day.

St Sunday Crag is often neglected in favour of Helvellyn and Striding Edge. This walk offers a less demanding approach, first travelling the length of the Grisedale valley before setting foot on the mountain.

These four summits are usually taken as part of the Kentmere Horseshoe and comprise one of the finest ridges of summits in the Lake District, while the long descent through Troutbeck is exquisite.

The summit of High Street used to be the scene of fairs and horse racing, and is crossed by the line of a Roman road. Combining the summit with nearby Harter Fell makes an excellent circuit.

| Always take with you: | | |
|---|---|---|
| ✔ warm, waterproof clothing | ✔ first-aid kit | ✔ compass |
| ✔ sufficient nourishing food | ✔ torch | ✔ relevant map |
| ✔ a hot drink | ✔ whistle | ✔ spare clothing |
| | ✔ mobile phone | ✔ spare batteries |

# About this guide

The context of the present book is reached by the stepping stones of earlier Pathfinder® guides by the publisher, books that seek to encourage those in the early stages of leisure walking by providing walks of increasing difficulty and daring. The High Fells of Lakeland goes one step further, inviting those who have gained experience in the many dales, around the lakes, and onto the easier routes up some of the major fells, to head for the tops, and to open up the whole of the Lake District to their exploration.

Each route leads to one or more fell summits, and requires the walker to be efficient in matters of map reading, use of compass and navigation, as detailed in the author's *Map Reading Skills*, also by Crimson Publishing. Almost all of the ascents in this book introduce the walker to some different aspect of fell wandering, whether a traverse of bleak moorland, a little rock scrambling, a touch of exposure here or a measure of remoteness there.

Unlike mainstream Pathfinder® guides, walks in the present book are not grouped into walks of increasing difficulty, but provide sufficient information for the walker to calculate for themselves the amount of time and effort likely to be needed. In this way, walkers will become more competent and more confident in their abilities.

Of course, you can equally take the book at face value, as a collection of walks to the top of some of Lakeland's most glorious high fells. And if you are into 'collecting' Marilyns, the Relative hills of Britain, then this book will take you up 15 of them.

# Keymap

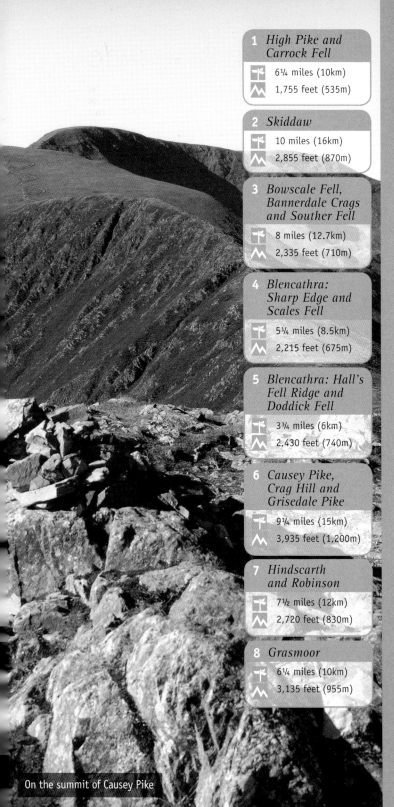

On the summit of Causey Pike

# North and North West Lakeland

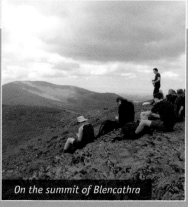

On the summit of Blencathra

The vast moorland area that lies beyond the barrier of Skiddaw and Blencathra is one of Lakeland's greatest delights but it is remote, and far from outside assistance. It is here that the adventurous walker will spend many happy hours, wandering the breezy fells and sauntering through deep-cleft valleys and across the oldest rocks on the very edge of Lakeland. Skiddaw may well rank as the most often ascended of all the Lakeland summits, drawing walkers who are lured by that elegant symmetry, which from the streets of Keswick is a challenge few walkers will ignore for long. Blencathra by contrast has enough routes to keep you occupied for a whole week without disappointment from simple grassy approaches to quite daunting rock edges and scrambles.

Beyond Keswick and across Bassenthwaite vale, the heights of afforested Whinlatter slip softly southwards over shapely Grisedale Pike and lush Coledale to the sensational ridge that runs from Rowling End and Causey Pike to Crag Hill, and then to bulky Grasmoor overlooking Crummock Water. Before slipping out of this north-west region, the Buttermere heights of Robinson and Hindscarth, soft, graceful summits with sufficient appeal will call you back again and again, rising from the exquisite Newlands valley on the one hand and bewitching Buttermere on the other. Crossing from one to the other, as you do at Newlands Hause, is a breathtaking moment, with fells soaring all around and the valley falling away at your feet.

The path up onto Sail

# High Pike and Carrock Fell

walk  1

*On a clear day the expansiveness about the curvaceous, grassy fells to the north of Blencathra and Skiddaw present no problem, but when the mist settles in it can be confusing. That aside, this is a splendid arena where you will encounter very few other walkers as you stride across a landscape bereft of trees and walls. En route you cross the most northerly of the Lakeland 600-metre summits.*

**Start**
Caldbeck Common, Mosedale

**Distance**
6¼ miles (10km)

**Height gain**
1,755 feet (535m)

**Route terrain**
Mine tracks; rough fell walking, moorland; loose rocks; very steep descent

**P Parking**
Off-road parking at site of Carrock End Mine

**OS maps**
Explorer OL5 (English Lakes – North-eastern area)

**GPS waypoints**
- NY 354 338
- Ⓐ NY 349 351
- Ⓑ NY 324 354
- Ⓒ NY 317 345
- Ⓓ NY 350 333

The walk begins from the site of the Carrock End Mine, along the road northwards from Mungrisdale and Mosedale. Where the focus of the old mine operations stood, there is ample off-road parking. The mine, which extracted copper, was never a major place of activity, and was last worked in 1869, although there is evidence that it existed more than 150 years earlier.

Set off northwards along the road, keeping left at a junction (or short-cutting it by an obvious track), and keep going until you cross Carrock Beck at a ford. A short way farther on, leave the road for a broad track Ⓐ running westwards above the beck.

The recess of Carrock Beck is very pleasant, sandwiched between the grassy slopes of West Fell and the more challenging slopes of Carrock Fell to the south. The old mine track runs the length of the valley, and when it divides, keep right rising steadily across the flank of West Fell to reach a widespread area of mining activity.

Pass through this and continue upwards to intercept a broad track Ⓑ arriving by a roundabout route from the hamlet of

*Heading for Carrock Fell*

Calebreck. This heads in a south-westerly direction, and does not go up to the summit of High Pike. So, immediately on having joined the track, leave it for a narrow path on the right rising across Low Pike to meet and turn left (south) onto a broad path that will lead you up to the top of the fell. On the way, you pass a northerly facing shelter before pressing on a little farther to the convenient bench, shelter and viewpoint trig pillar that marks the summit of High Pike.

The view from the summit is quite special, exposing a fine panorama that ranges from the highest of the Pennines and across the Cumbrian Plain and Solway Firth to the Southern Uplands of Scotland.

From the top of High Pike, set off southwards, following a descending path that shortly intercepts the track encountered earlier **C**. Cross this and follow a clear path around the top of Drygill Beck, later swinging more easterly as you follow a boggy path across Miton Hill. From here you can make a beeline for the prominent cairn on Carrock Fell, but there is slightly drier and firmer ground if you deviate in a south-easterly direction to the low rocky upthrusts of Round Knott, and head up onto the rocky summit of Carrock Fell from there.

From the top of Carrock Fell continue eastwards, passing more clearly through the hill fort perimeter, and continuing to a cairn on the very edge of Carrock End. Here the path changes direction, heading south east, and begins falling steeply. There is a

> ### John Peel
> The Caldbeck fells were the happy hunting ground of John Peel, born in the nearby village of Caldbeck in 1776, and one of 13 children. He and his wife, the 18-year-old daughter of a wealthy farmer from Uldale, were married at Gretna Green after his future mother-in-law objected to their marriage. In the end, begrudgingly, the family accepted that the two were indeed married, but insisted on a service of remarriage at Caldbeck church.
>
> Peel started hunting with his own pack of hounds, and, in the traditional Lakeland manner, often followed them on foot. He is forever immortalised in the verses of *D'ye ken John Peel*.

clear path all the way, but tread carefully. On the way, you pass an old ruined shelter. The target is the ravine

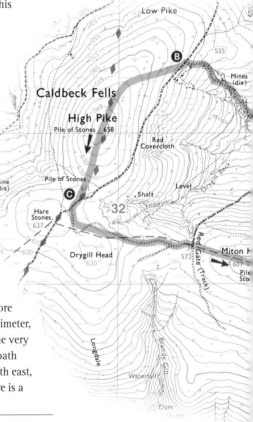

of Further Gill Sike **D**, and the descending path (not shown on maps until it enters the ravine), in places, narrow and through heather, leads directly to it.

As you enter the top of the ravine, the path is deep cut into a channel, but this is short-lived, and you soon enter the top of the ravine itself. *The way down is now unremittingly steep*, initially on grass or loose stones. *At no time should you relax your concentration here*, other than to sit down and admire the view over the limestone pastures of Greystoke to the distant Pennines.

Lower down you meet the watercourse itself, and continue descending until the path clearly branches left (north-east) and begins a downward diagonal traverse first of scree, then across bracken slopes until the path runs out into close-cropped turf close by the starting point.

## Carrock Fell

Here on Carrock Fell, Skiddaw Slates, the oldest rocks in Lakeland, butt up against igneous rocks that have yielded copper ore and other minerals. Above Carrock End, the crags at the eastern edge of the fell also contain black gabbro, the rock of the Skye Cuillin, which is rare in Lakeland. Above all else Carrock Fell is unique in having a vast ancient hill fort on its summit. Its origins are unclear but the extent of the collapsed walls that circle the top of the fell suggest that the fort must have been a large and important stronghold.

SCALE 1:25 000 or 2½ INCHES to 1 MILE 4CM to 1KM

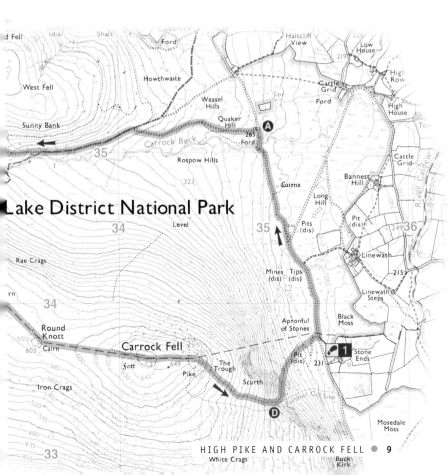

# walk 2

# *Skiddaw*

**Start**

Underscar (top of Gale Road)

**Distance**

10 miles (16km)

**Height gain**

2,855 feet (870m)

**Route terrain**

Rough fell walking, steep descent, moorland tracks

**P Parking**

Roadside parking at start

**OS maps**

Explorer OL4 (English Lakes – North-western area)

**GPS waypoints**

NY 281 253
Ⓐ NY 271 275
Ⓑ NY 260 290
Ⓒ NY 272 313
Ⓓ NY 287 291

*The ascent of Skiddaw, the sixth highest summit in the Lake District, is documented from the 17th century. The mountain dominates the town of Keswick, a challenge that few can resist. Most visitors content themselves with a simple up-and-down conquest, but this walk extends the experience by traversing the mountain and descending to the delightful area known as Back o'Skidda'.*

Gale Road, at the top of which the ascent begins, is reached via Ormathwaite or Applethwaite, and climbs steadily, if roughly, as a deteriorating road to a broad col linking the mass of Skiddaw with the nearby Latrigg. From here go through a gate/stile and turn left onto a gravel path beside a wall, which later swings round to a gate, beyond which a gentle rise leads up to a monument to three shepherds of the Hawell family, noted for their skill in breeding the ubiquitous Herdwick sheep of Lakeland.

Beyond the monument, the long slope of Jenkin Hill awaits, an obvious, trail leading unendingly upwards.

## Skiddaw

Starting in Keswick, this was the first tourist route up Skiddaw, an undertaking described by local Harriet Martineau as '...easy, even for ladies, who have only to sit their ponies to find themselves at the top, after a ride of six miles.' Another contemporary writer recommended taking a guide along with '...sandwiches and brandy, to recruit their strength previous to the descent.' There is evidence that one party at least (including the Wordsworth and Southey families), who had climbed Skiddaw to light a bonfire in celebration of the victory at Waterloo, came down all the merrier when Wordsworth accidentally kicked over the water compelling everyone to drink neat rum to assuage their thirst.

The way up Jenkin Hill has seen repair work in recent years and succumbs to a steady plod. Eventually the gradient relaxes as the double-topped summit of Little Man, a precursor to Skiddaw itself, eases into view. By the time you reach a gate in a fence Ⓐ *you have the option of keeping to the west of it and taking in Little Man (adding 410 feet to the height gain, but little or nothing to the overall distance).* Otherwise press on along the main trail, and as the terrain becomes more and more

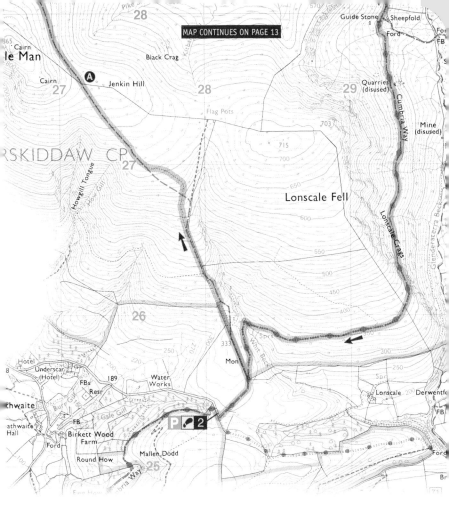

MAP CONTINUES ON PAGE 13

0   200   400   600   800 METRES   1
0   200   400   600 YARDS   ½
KILOMETRES
MILES

stony under foot, you finally pull up through another gate onto the raised ridge that leads to the summit of the fell **B**. In poor visibility, the summit, marked by cairns, shelters and a trig pillar, will be a disappointment; but on a clear day quite the opposite, offering a magnificent panorama, especially to the south, into the heart of Lakeland.

*(Many walkers retreat from the summit, and head back down, and there is no disgrace in doing just that; although if that is your plan you might consider starting the walk at the disused railway station car park in Keswick and*

Looking back to Skiddaw House from Salehow Beck

There is, understandably, a great sense of remoteness in the heart of the northern fells. Skiddaw seems to lie back and does not hold the same appeal from the east. The same cannot be said of Lonscale Fell, a southerly outlier of Skiddaw but with a stupendous eastern face, across which the onward route passes as a most delightful terraced path high above Glenderaterra Beck. This is a magical place; so few come this way, Cumbria Way notwithstanding.

*walking up via Spooney Green Lane from there. To take this option and start in Keswick would give a walk of 9¼ miles (14.8km), with 2,885 feet (880m) of height gain.)*

Continue across the summit of Skiddaw, following a clear path. Gradually you close in on a fence on your right, and then as you do so the path seems to end close by a couple of low cairns. Now simply walk towards the fence and follow it. When the fence changes direction, stay beside it and start descending to the outlying minor summit, Bakestall. As you descend, the view opens up of the grass and heather hills of Great Calva, Knott and the distant Caldbeck Fells. A brief diversion takes you out to the cairn on Bakestall, which proves to be a lovely viewpoint, looking north to the Solway Firth and the hills of lowland Scotland.

Keep following the fence as it descends steeply from Bakestall, the descending path bringing you down to intercept the Cumbria Way at the top of Whitewater Dash **C**, a spectacular waterfall best seen from the north. As you reach the Way, turn right through a gate to follow a broad track to cross Dash Beck, and then begin the long and glorious traverse of the moors towards the distant hostel at Skiddaw House **D**, on the way crossing the

*Skiddaw and Jenkin Hill from Latrigg*

infant River Caldew.

Just after Skiddaw House you cross Salehow Beck to a gate, and then a grassy slope before taking to a gently rising track across the lower slopes of Lonscale Fell. Make the most of the traverse, it is quite splendid and easy to negotiate, but tread carefully on a short rocky section towards the end.

Eventually, you leave this section as you round the southern slopes of Lonscale Fell. But now you press on to enter one of Lakeland's most charming nooks as you dance across bridgeless Whit Beck. Only a short pull now remains to take you back up towards the Hawell monument and the top of Gale Road.

**Start**

Mungrisdale

**Distance**

8 miles (12.7km)

**Height gain**

2,335 feet (710m)

**Route terrain**

Stony tracks, fell and moorland paths

**P Parking**

Roadside parking area (Honesty payment) opposite the Recreation Rooms

**OS maps**

Explorer OL5 (English Lakes – North-eastern area)

**GPS waypoints**

📍 NY 364 302
Ⓐ NY 356 302
Ⓑ NY 344 298
Ⓒ NY 332 302
Ⓓ NY 327 291
Ⓔ NY 343 279
Ⓕ NY 354 291

# Bowscale Fell, Bannerdale Crags and Souther Fell

*Bannerdale Crags will never attract the rock-climbing fraternity, they are too crumbly and shaly for that, but they do have quite a shapely profile when viewed from the adjacent Souther Fell. Elsewhere the route visits the source of the River Glenderamackin and a grassy fell once inhabited by a spectral army. But the walk begins with what is generally regarded as the easiest Lakeland 2,000 feet-summit to achieve, Bowscale Fell.*

📍 Set off by crossing the bridge over the Glenderamackin and walk up to pass to the left of the **Mill Inn**, an ancient dog-friendly inn, probably 17th-century, and later a coaching inn, today perfectly poised for a post-perambulatory pint or bowl of soup.

> **Mungrisdale** The remote hamlet of Mungrisdale is a tiny community whose name is believed to derive from the Old Norse 'Grisadalr', the valley of the pigs; the addition of 'Mung' came later and is of uncertain meaning. The nearby church, however, is dedicated to St Kentigern, who was also known as Mungo, and a man who was bishop of Glasgow in the 6th century. The church was built in 1756 of simple design with thick rubble stone walls, although an earlier building, marked as a chapel on maps, had been on the same site. Inside the present church is a memorial to a young and frail Raisley Calvert, a friend and benefactor of William Wordsworth.

Turn right at the rear of the inn, and follow a narrow lane out to rejoin the valley road you just left. A few strides farther on, branch left past the telephone box and along a broad track (signposted for Mungrisdale Common).

Once you pass through a gate, you are faced with a wide expanse of rough pasture, and, directly ahead and perhaps a little intimidating, the pyramidal fell known as The Tongue. It's actually an easterly extension of Bowscale Fell, and the route passes easily to its left. So, go forward, following a stony track until, as the Glenderamackin changes direction you can cross a narrow footbridge Ⓐ spanning Bullfell Beck. Here keep to the

Looking across from the summit of Bannerdale Crags to Souther Fell and the distant Pennines

main track, rising gently, ignoring a branching path, less distinct, along the course of the Glenderamackin.

The gradient is quite uniform, but frequent pauses to gaze down the valley of the Glenderamackin and across the steep eastern face of Bannerdale Crags will soon bring you to a point where the track again forks **B**. Keep right, taking the higher path, which soon steepens a little as it approaches the rim of Bannerdale.

From the top of the ascending path, leave the rim path, by going forward across short turf on a narrow grassy path. *Off to your right, you can see the top of Bowscale Fell, and at any time you can make a beeline for it, crossing untracked ground. Otherwise, for rather easier going, keep heading roughly west, and just beyond a low finger of rock you intercept another path* **C**. Here, there is a lovely view extending from Blencathra to the south, across Skiddaw to Great Calva, Raise, High Pike and Carrock Fell. At the cross path, turn right, heading east of north, and stroll up to the top of Bowscale Fell.

Having visited Bowscale Fell, topped by a large pile of rocks, turn around and head back down to that cross-path **C**. Continue heading roughly in a southerly direction, but soon the path divides. Now bear left across rough ground until you reach the rim of the fell above Bannerdale. There is a good path now, and this leads gently upwards in a south-easterly direction to the top

**River Glenderamackin** This brief but delightful river at some stage flows in every direction, north, south, east and west, but only as far as Threlkeld, where it becomes the River Greta. Its name is of uncertain derivation but likely of Brythonic origin from 'glyndwfr mochyn', meaning 'the river valley of the pigs', similar in fact to the derivation of Mungrisdale.

of Bannerdale Crags. A large cairn marks the popular top of the fell, with a lovely view east across Souther Fell to the distant Pennines and Cross Fell.

The cairn, however, is not the highest point of the fell; this lies a short distance to the west, and a broad grassy trod leads you that way. The true summit is marked by a rather dismal, flattened cairn, but the whole scene here is dominated by the sprawling bulk of Blencathra, which from this angle shows why it has the alternative name of 'Saddleback'.

From the cairn, continue roughly north-westwards following a now descending quad bike track. Follow the path to its lowest point on a col **D** overlooking Mungrisdale Common. Here, turn left (south-east), taking the lower of two paths that leads down to the headwaters of the River Glenderamackin. A short way down the path you meet a spring that is the primary source of the river.

The path down the valley is a delight to follow, hemmed in on both sides by steep-sided grassy fell slopes, which, to the west, lead up into the hollow containing Scales Tarn above which rises the narrow rocky crest of Sharp Edge, one of the slimmest and airiest

mountain ridges in Lakeland.

Eventually, as you follow the descending path, you reach a point where a narrow path branches right, down to a footbridge **E** spanning the river. Go this way, cross the bridge, and climb the path beyond.

The path leads to a broad grassy col beyond which lies Mousthwaite Comb, but you do not go quite that far. Once on the col, almost immediately you encounter a cross-path. Here, turn left, and climb steadily onto the grassy slopes of Souther Fell.

When the on-going path forks, *you can take either route; the one on the right keeping to the high ground, the*

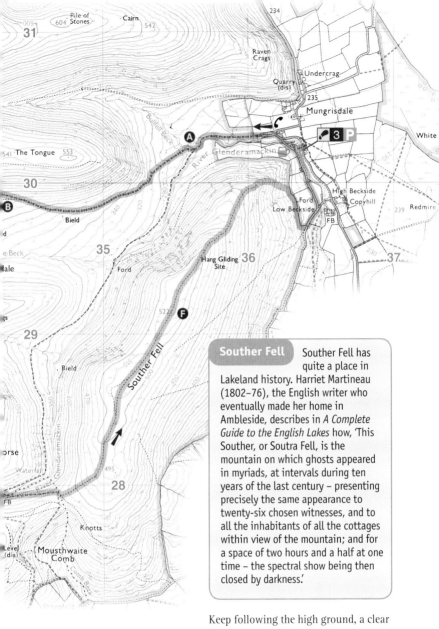

**Souther Fell** Souther Fell has quite a place in Lakeland history. Harriet Martineau (1802–76), the English writer who eventually made her home in Ambleside, describes in *A Complete Guide to the English Lakes* how, 'This Souther, or Soutra Fell, is the mountain on which ghosts appeared in myriads, at intervals during ten years of the last century – presenting precisely the same appearance to twenty-six chosen witnesses, and to all the inhabitants of all the cottages within view of the mountain; and for a space of two hours and a half at one time – the spectral show being then closed by darkness.'

one on the left heading for a large cairn from which there is a fine view of your line of ascent along Bannerdale Rigg, and north to Bowscale Fell. A path leads from the cairn back to the high ground.

The summit of the fell **F** is a bit of an anticlimax, a small shaly outcrop with no other distinguishing feature.

Keep following the high ground, a clear path leading you to the end of the fell, where the path drops in stages to one final steep flourish. Stay with it as far as a waymark post, and here turn right following a narrow path that leads down to meet a wall. Turn right beside the wall, and then, later, at a fence corner you can turn left and descend to meet a lane at a gate. Through the gate follow the lane, which will lead you back to the Mill Inn.

# walk 4

**Start**
Scales

**Distance**
5¼ miles (8.5km)

**Height gain**
2,215 feet (675m)

**Route terrain**
Rough fell walking, craggy outcrops, mild scrambling (avoidable); *Sharp Edge is difficult in winter conditions*

**P Parking**
Roadside parking alongside A66

**OS maps**
Explorer OL5 (English Lakes – North-eastern area)

**GPS waypoints**
📍 NY 343 269
Ⓐ NY 348 272
Ⓑ NY 347 274
Ⓒ NY 344 278
Ⓓ NY 329 281
Ⓔ NY 329 277
Ⓕ NT 343 277
Ⓖ NT 345 273

# Blencathra: Sharp Edge and Scales Fell

*Blencathra is one of those summits you can ascend by a different route almost every day of the week and never tire of doing so. The most direct route is by Hall's Fell Ridge (Walk 5), but the ascent by Sharp Edge is the most exciting, involving as it does a measure of mild rock scrambling.*

📍 The walk sets off from the hamlet of Scales, passing the **White Horse Inn**. Immediately after the inn, branch left onto a narrow lane. Follow the lane for 650 yds until, just after it starts to descend and before a pronounced bend, you can leave it at a signpost on the left for a path to Blackhazle Beck Ⓐ. You soon pass through a kissing-gate beyond which rises the great green hollow of Mousthwaite Comb, the terminus of Souther Fell.

The on-going path climbs steadily into the comb, flanked mostly by bracken. When the path forks Ⓑ, keep ahead, targeting the lower end of a splendid slanting rake that slashes across the upper section of the Comb at an easy angle. The walk up the rake is quite delightful and offers fine views southwards to the hummocky line of the Dodds in particular.

At the top of the rake, the path swings to the left (west) as it reaches the grassy col linking Scales Fell and Souther Fell; directly ahead lies the grassy rump of Bannerdale Crags, and a little to the left your objective, Sharp Edge. Follow the wide grassy path in the direction of Scales Fell, but before really getting to grips with the fell, branch right Ⓒ onto a near horizontal path high above the infant River Glenderamackin.

The path is a lovely stroll, virtually flat, relaxing after the climb through Mousthwaite Comb, and with Sharp Edge looming ever closer. Eventually, the path swings to the left and climbs beside Scales Beck, which has been stepped in recent years. The ascent is brief, crossing the beck on boulders and passing a rowan that has seen better years. Even at the top of the beck, Scales Tarn refuses to come into view until the very last moment. But when it does, what a splendid setting it enjoys with the tilted boilerplate slabs that culminate in Sharp

Saddleb

32

Edge on the right, and the upper slopes of Blencathra directly ahead. This is quite superb, and an ideal place to take a break. Scales Tarn **D** is a classic corrie tarn, gathering all the water from this great bowl and channelling it in Scales Beck and ultimately down into the River Glenderamackin.

*Walkers who decide against tackling Sharp Edge should here cross the outflow of the tarn to gain a clear ascending path that takes them to within striking distance of the summit.*

To the east of the tarn, a stony path ascends to the base of Sharp Edge. For the ascent (some 600 yds) you will need to use your hands.

*Heading for Sharp Edge*

Sharp Edge divides into two sections: the first is a fairly low-angled crest of a rocky ridge, followed by a steeper pull up rock to the edge of Atkinson Pike. The initial part is avoidable by a path

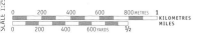

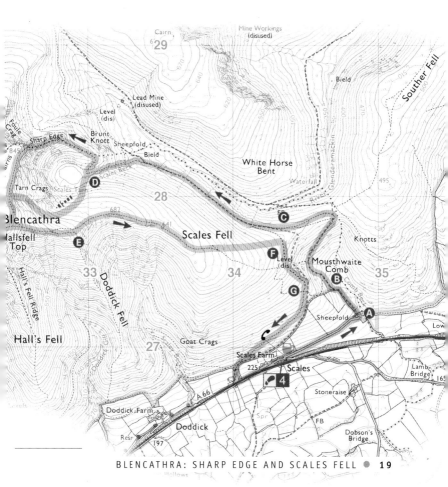

on the right-hand (north) side of the ridge, but it is arguably better to favour the crest to which you will have to ascend eventually, not least because the view is much better.

Above the narrow col a clear, shallow gully can be seen striking up the slope, slightly left of vertical. You can manoeuvre into this from the narrow col, and it will provide secure hand- and footholds as you gain height, fairly enclosed and so largely devoid of any sense of exposure. Once this gully expires you are close to the top and can continue on good holds to gain a horizontal, shaly path.

Having gained the path it is worth taking a moment to walk up to the top of Foule Crag, known as Atkinson Pike to take in the view over Mungrisdale Common and because it is this slight uplift that serves with Blencathra itself to give the distinctive profile that earns the mountain its alternative name, Saddleback (best seen from the approach from the east along the A66).

Follow the shaly path towards the top of Blencathra, on the way joining the ascending Scales Fell path. The top of the mountain has little to distinguish it, apart from the outstanding view; a countersunk trig point and a modest cairn gather at the highest point.

The descent is via Scales Fell, and sets off by retracing the path towards Sharp Edge, but after only 100 yds the path divides. Take that on the right, with Scales Fell and now the upper reaches of Doddick Fell in view. The path zigzags down and crosses the top of Doddick Fell **E**, with more zigzags to follow before a clear path runs on along the edge of Scales Fell, high above the upper reaches of Scaley Beck.

As you descend Scales Fell, the path moves away from Scaley Beck, and swings to the north east, heading for the linking col with Souther Fell crossed on the ascent. Before rejoining your outward route, you intercept a cross-path at a small embedded rock **F**. Here turn right to discover that the path becomes very narrow as it crosses the top of old mine workings, but then relaxes and passes on through extensive bracken to a path junction **G**. Keep forward, with the path now changing direction to south and south-west as it descends steadily through bracken finally to reach a kissing-gate above a short and final descent to the A66; turn left to complete the walk. ●

Scales Fell

# Blencathra: Hall's Fell Ridge and Doddick Fell

*There is a widely held view that to ascend Blencathra by Hall's Fell Ridge is one of the finest, if not the finest, route to the summit of any of the Lake District fells. It is certainly very direct. This is energetic walking from the off; a rite of passage for ambitious fell wanderers.*

### Start
Threlkeld

### Distance
3¾ miles (6km)

### Height gain
2,430 feet (740m)

### Route terrain
Rough fell walking, craggy outcrops, scree; *difficult in winter conditions*

### Parking
Limited roadside parking in village; car park at NY 318256

### OS maps
Explorer OL5 (English Lakes – North-eastern area)

### GPS waypoints
NY 324 255
**A** NY 324 261
**B** NY 323 277
**C** NY 329 277

The ascent starts in the village of Threlkeld, famed for its huntsmen, many of whom are named and remembered on a monument in the churchyard.

The village is now by-passed by the A66, but soon after leaving the A-road, turn right onto a minor back road (Fell Side) that leads to a bridleway on the left leading up to Gategill Farm **A**. On reaching the farm, pass through a gate into the farmyard, walking between buildings to a double gate that gives onto an enclosed pathway above the narrow ravine and cascades of Gate Gill.

As you walk on, a stunning and daunting view suddenly appears of Hall's Fell Top rising above the as yet unseen recesses of Gate Gill. The path leads to another gate and beyond bears right, across Gate Gill, in the vicinity of the disused Woodend Lead Mine.

### Threlkeld (Woodend) Lead Mine

The Threlkeld Lead Mine functioned in the late 19th and early 20th century, being highly productive, yielding large quantities of lead and zinc, between 1879 and 1928, although the workings date back to the 17th century.

Once across the stream, plod steadily up a steeply ascending path through bracken, heather and low rock outcrops to gain a foothold on the broad base of Hall's Fell ridge. The onward route is not in doubt, but the going is steep and frequent rest halts are advised, ostensibly to let you take in the richness of the valley fields below, the ever-widening panorama of Great and Little Mell Fells, and the hazy, purple fells around Derwentwater.

*Blencathra, late evening*

After what seems like a long haul, the gradient eases, and the ridge begins to narrow, at first only marginally so, but then more dramatically, as Doddick Fell and the bulkier Scales Fell come into view. A wide outcrop of rock spanning the width of the ridge marks the start of the section known as Narrow Edge, a succession of shapely outcrops, mini-towers, gullies and ledges that walkers adept at scrambling will find pleasure in tackling head on. Less confident walkers will find a way round for much of the ascent on one side or other of the ridge, though in the end it becomes easier to deal with the ridge than to try avoiding it.

The great beauty of the ridge is that it leads unerringly to the summit **B**, largely undistinguished except for a modest cairn just below the high point and a countersunk OS trig pillar. The view, not surprisingly, is outstanding, and reaches far into the heart of Lakeland as well as northwards and

north-west to the lower Northern Fells and Skiddaw.

The continuation to Doddick Fell leaves the summit briefly in a north-easterly direction, as if heading for the conspicuous point of Atkinson Pike at the top of Sharp Edge, but as the stony path divides bear right to find that the on-going path descends in wide zigzags. To the left, Sharp Edge eases into view above as yet unseen Scales Tarn, while beyond rise the low mounds of Bannerdale Crags and Bowscale Fell.

The descending path is bound for Scales Fell, but en route passes the top of Doddick Fell, identified by two prominent craggy upthrusts **C**. Between the two it becomes possible to leave the main path and move right onto a narrow trod starting down the flank of Doddick Fell, although it is arguably easier to continue along the Scales Fell path for a little while longer, tackling more zigzags and, as these end, leaving the path at a low, collapsed cairn on the right. The start of the way down Doddick Fell from either point eventually takes to a narrow shaly path flirting with rock outcrops, maintaining a steepness that calls for caution for some way down the ridge.

The continuation down the ridge is a pleasure to walk. It gives fine views of Clough Head and Great Dodd across the Vale of Keswick, and Hall's Fell Top in particular, as it passes through a rash of heather before arriving at a final outcrop immediately beyond which the ridge broadens and plummets to the buildings and green pastures of Doddick Farm.

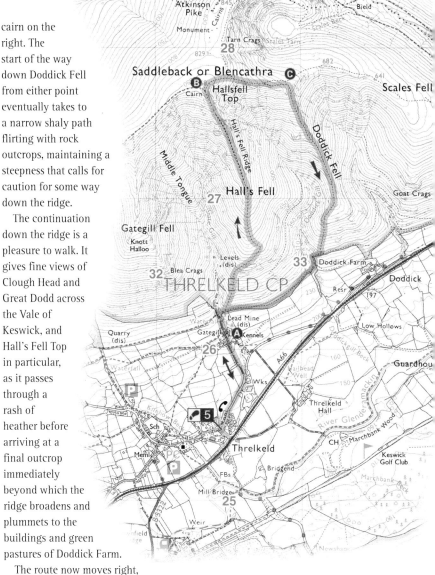

The route now moves right, descending gradually to reach the intake wall not far east of Doddick Gill. Follow the path, right, alongside the wall and when it starts to move away, towards the gill, stay with the wall to its end, there turning left to drop down to cross the gill at a ford. A good path leads on then above the on-going intake wall, and pleasantly across the base of Hall's Fell ridge back to Gate Gill near the Woodend mine, from where you simply retrace your outward steps to Threlkeld.

Of interest, especially for those who enjoy a little refreshment at the end of a walk, is the **Horse and Farrier** pub, one of the oldest in the Lake District, built in 1688, and sometime refreshment stop for Wordsworth as he travelled between Grasmere and Penrith undertaking his duties as postmaster.

SCALE 1:25000 or 2½ INCHES to 1 MILE 4CM to 1KM

# walk 6

## Start
Stoneycroft

## Distance
9¼ miles (15km)

## Height gain
3,935 feet (1,200m)

## Route terrain
Rough fell walking, craggy outcrops, scree

## Parking
Limited roadside parking at various points

## OS maps
Explorer OL4 (English Lakes – North-western area)

## GPS waypoints
- NY 233 222
- **A** NY 222 207
- **B** NY 204 205
- **C** NY 189 213
- **D** NY 232 235

# Causey Pike, Crag Hill and Grisedale Pike

*The ability to combine a number of high fells into one walk is ably demonstrated in this circuit of Coledale. Once you reach the first summit, Causey Pike, a delightful broad ridge of fells follows before you need to lose height. It is a perfect walk for a fine day, but has a couple of built-in escape routes should the weather deteriorate. There is special appeal too, in the wide and ever-changing panorama that accompanies you all the way.*

There are a number of places to park along the Newlands road, running south from Braithwaite, and from here, walk along the road to Stoneycroft, there crossing Stoneycroft Gill. A few strides farther on, leave the road for a flight of steps (low signpost) on the right, giving onto a clear footpath that rises westwards across the slopes of Rowling End. The ascent is gradual, but the views at this stage confined by the bulk of Barrow.

Ahead you will see the enticing rocky cone of Causey Pike. As you approach the col **A** linking Causey Pike with Rowling End, the path zigzags a little before reaching the col, marked by a low cairn. The immediate prospect is of the Newlands valley at the head of which rise Dalehead, Hindscarth and Robinson, backed by the High Stile ridge above Buttermere.

Turning to face Causey Pike it is clear that the onward route

*On the summit of Causey Pike*

Crag Hill from Sail

is rocky. Stony paths draw you up through heather and bracken, but finally you reach the foot of a rock barrier. Rock scrambling is now called for, because no one (surely) could walk up the next few feet with their hands in their pockets (nor is that an incitement to try!). The scrambling is delightful, and the many ways well polished: such difficulties as there are should deter no one. Then suddenly, you pop out onto the top of the fell to be greeted by the rippling series of humps that give Causey Pike its distinct profile, running westward into the fells of Scar Crags, Sail and ultimately Crag Hill, the highest point of the circuit.

A clear path now crosses the remaining summits, undulating along Causey Pike before dipping a little to begin the easy pull onto Scar Crags, which is surprisingly (but not worryingly) narrow. As you progress along Scar Crags, so the next fell, Sail, eases into view. But it is the path up onto Sail that will draw your attention, a long series of zigzags that replace the

hitherto direct and unvarying line. This circuit has always been popular, and the new path merely suggests that the old one must have become badly eroded.

The path descending from Scar Crags has had a little of the same treatment, and it comes down to a clear cross-path **B**, the first line of escape (northwards) following a clear path round into the valley housing Stoneycroft Gill. From this crossing point, the on-going path is blindingly obvious and enables you to sail up Sail. After the excitement of the ascent, the grassy top of Sail is something of a disappointment, its highest point marked by a tiny cairn. Onward, however, looms the bulk of Crag Hill, reached by a narrowing ridge that completes the ascent to the trig pillar on the summit. Directly to the west lies Grasmoor, an enormous mound of a fell, but not as appealing as Crag Hill, which is more central and has the better panorama.

The next objective is Coledale Hause, a high mountain pass, wonderfully surrounded by soaring fellsides. This col lies west of north from Crag Hill, but a direct line, over Eel Crag, is not advised as it leads only into an abomination of scree. Instead, set off from the summit by going west, to the link with Grasmoor, there turning northwards on a good path beside the upper reaches of Lisa Beck. As you approach the hause, another escape route lies eastwards, down a broad clear path that leads to Force Crag Mine and out to Braithwaite. Go this way if you cannot face up to Grisedale Pike.

Take care to locate the path **C**, which slants up towards Grisedale Pike, passing first over an un-named companion, and with improving views of the fragile cliffs of Hobcarton Crags east of shapely Hopegill Head. The way up onto Grisedale Pike is obvious, rising steadily to a slaty summit.

From the summit, the descent takes to the north-east ridge, Sleet How. There is an initial steep descent to gain the ridge, but then a clear path runs down onto a lower section and finally

**Braithwaite** Braithwaite today is a quiet place with few residents employed locally, but in the past it had more than 1,000 inhabitants and its own coterie of trades people – butcher, baker, blacksmiths, millers, shoemaker, grocer, joiners and builders – and was closely associated with the village of Thornthwaite to the north. Formerly the seat of a thriving woollen industry, Braithwaite was the first location of the Cumberland Pencil Company formed in 1868, a business that only moved to its site in Keswick 30 years later when the buildings burned down.

emerging on the Whinlatter road, a short distance above the village of Braithwaite.

Walk down to the village. Cross the first bridge that you come to, and immediately turn left, passing cottages to reach another bridge. Here, keep right along the Newlands road, but shortly leave it at a broad track **D** up to Braithwaite Lodge, continuing beyond the Lodge and keeping above a small area of woodland, eventually to emerge on the Newlands road not far north of your starting point.

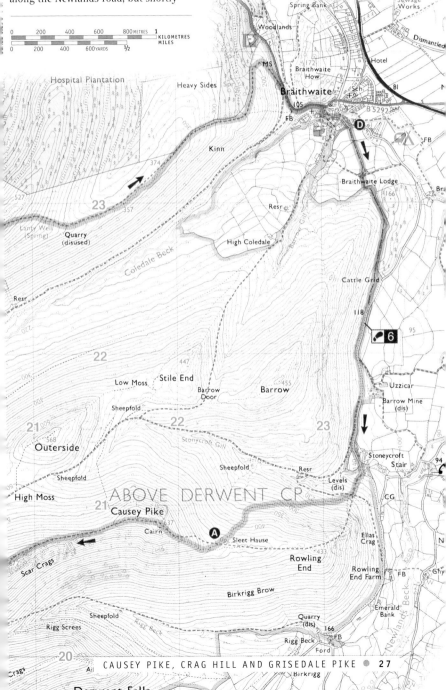

# walk 7

## Start
Newlands valley

## Distance
7½ miles (12km)

## Height gain
2,720 feet (830m)

## Route terrain
Minor roads, high fell tracks and paths, rugged and rocky fell summits

## Parking
Small parking area, near Rigg Beck

## OS maps
Explorer OL4 (English Lakes – North-western area)

## GPS waypoints
- NY 229 201
- **Ⓐ** NY 229 193
- **Ⓑ** NY 225 184
- **Ⓒ** NY 213 160
- **Ⓓ** NY 202 169
- **Ⓔ** NY 220 186

# Hindscarth and Robinson

*Lying south-west of Derwentwater, the Newlands valley is shaped by one of the smallest groups of fells in the Lake District, but one that boasts two splendid ridges, roughly at right angles, and a fine selection of shapely summits. The underlying rocks are Skiddaw Slates, revealing themselves in the smooth shape of the fells, the general absence of tarns, and a vegetation mainly of grass and heather. This walk visits two of the fells, accompanied by fine views throughout.*

The walk begins at Rigg Beck where a disused quarry accommodates a few cars. From it, set off up the valley road and almost immediately turn left to pass the site of a building (Rigg Beck) popularly known as the Purple House. This landmark property, originally built in the 1880s as a hotel fell into disrepair in 2007, and a year later was burned down. In its time it was a lodging house for actors at Keswick Theatre, an assembly that included the likes of Bob Hoskins, Victoria Wood and poet Ted Hughes. It was always intended to replace Rigg Beck, and a magnificent building in the vernacular style now takes its place as a private residence.

Go past Rigg Beck and follow quiet lanes leading to Newlands Chapel **Ⓐ**. Take the track on the left, just past the chapel, and follow this to Low Snab Farm.

Along this initial road-walking section as far as Low Snab, the exquisite beauty of the Newlands valley is overwhelming. There is a melancholic loveliness about the dale: green pastures bordered by ancient hawthorn, willow, ash, sycamore and oak, and dotted with isolated farmsteads that might once have housed the 'estatesmen' farmers described by Wordsworth, and whom he almost certainly had in mind when he described the dale as 'By few but shepherds trod'. The red squirrel is here, too, sharing the treetops with jays, thrushes, cuckoos, pipits, and a variety of tits. There is a peaceful calm about the place leading you on beyond the

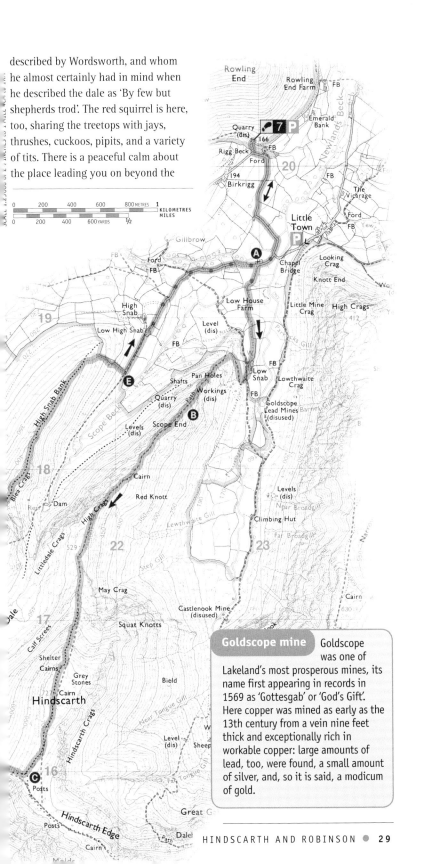

### Goldscope mine

Goldscope was one of Lakeland's most prosperous mines, its name first appearing in records in 1569 as 'Gottesgab' or 'God's Gift'. Here copper was mined as early as the 13th century from a vein nine feet thick and exceptionally rich in workable copper: large amounts of lead, too, were found, a small amount of silver, and, so it is said, a modicum of gold.

*Robinson and Hindscarth from above Buttermere*

on, lies the summit of the fell, marked by a cairn in the middle of a vast stony plateau.

Press on from the summit along a cairned path leading south to a small prominence **C** on which appears a clear pathway. *(If you turn left at this point, easy walking will take you to the summit of Dalehead. From there you will need to retrace your steps. This additional 1½ miles is not included in the walk distance.)*

If not visiting Dalehead, turn right, and descend to a col, before ascending again, to a large cairn. Now you must turn north across stony ground to reach the summit of Robinson **D**, a fine fell named after a local worthy, Richard Robinson, who purchased it during the reign of Henry VIII as monastic properties were coming up for sale.

The top of Robinson can be confusing in poor visibility, but the way off lies north-north-east, keeping well away from the north-facing Robinson Crags and tending rather more towards Little Dale, the valley between Robinson and Hindscarth. A clear path leads down, but on the way you pass through a couple of small rock bands that will call for the use of hands and, perhaps, a well-placed bottom before you reach the easier ground of High Snab Bank.

High above High Snab Farm, a steep flourish takes you down towards Scope Beck, before reaching which you turn onto a path **E** towards the farm and follow its access lane out as far as Newlands Chapel, where you join your outward route.

farm and through a gate onto the open fellside.

Ahead lies Hindscarth, the shapeliest of summits, its great tilted peak and adjacent ridge stark and blatant against the sky, a challenge to any walker. Nearby are the waste spills of the Goldscope Mine, another section of which can be seen across the valley.

Follow the wall behind Low Snab Farm for a short distance, and then climb left onto Scope End **B**. For a time now the going is steep and energetic, but there is a clear path, and when the initial pull is completed, with the whole ridge to Hindscarth stretching before you, the brilliance of the setting easily overcomes any fatigue.

Continue along the ridge, rising steadily. It narrows in a few places, but is never intimidating. The path gambols up and down, switching from one side of the ridge to the other, until you arrive at the foot of the final, steep haul to the summit. Now a low gear and a steady plod is the best way to deal with this final uphill stretch, which, in spite of its off-putting appearance, is soon completed, and you find yourself beside a circular shelter that has been in view for some time. A short distance farther

# Grasmoor

*From the east, the bulk of Grasmoor resembles a whale breaking the surface of the sea, while closer inspection seems to invite nothing but toil. Yet few would disagree that the ascent via the Lad Hows ridge is superb, a great curving sweep rising from the valley floor, from where Lad Hows appears as a separate fell. Ascend this way, and you are treated to a day on the fells with few equals. Here, the walk is linked with fells to the south-east to add glory to an already splendid outing.*

 Begin from the parking area by heading through a gate and bearing right to a footbridge spanning Squat Beck. Then go left along a track and past a gate until you spot a path Ⓐ branching uphill, and then diagonally left through bracken to a shoulder overlooking Cinderdale Beck. Here you about face and continue climbing onto the end of the Lad Hows ridge, arrival at which is marked by a cairn.

Only now does the true shape of Lad Hows come into perspective, rising through heather, the gradient never relaxing much, but the path remaining straightforward as it rises in a majestic sweep to a moderate cairn on the edge of Grasmoor's summit plateau. Not far away lies a multi-directional shelter that marks the top of the fell Ⓑ. The summit plateau is grassy with patches of bare slate, and with a scattering of mostly unhelpful cairns. A small shelter-cairn overlooking Crummock Water is a fine vantage point, however.

## walk 8

**Start**
Rannerdale (Crummock Water)

**Distance**
6¼ miles (10km)

**Height gain**
3,135 feet (955m)

**Route terrain**
Steep and rough fell walking, craggy outcrops, scree

**Parking**
Hause Point

**OS maps**
Explorer OL4 (English Lakes – North-western area)

**GPS waypoints**
🖉 NY 163 183
Ⓐ NY 165 189
Ⓑ NY 175 203
Ⓒ NY 188 201
Ⓓ NY 188 197
Ⓔ NY 181 191

*Wandope from Sail*

*Grasmoor group from above Buttermere*

*Those wanting to visit Grasmoor only may simply return by the upward route.* Otherwise, the continuation lies eastwards, following a line of cairns until a clear path comes into view, leading down to the col linking Grasmoor with Crag Hill. From the col, where there is usually a couple of tiny tarns, bear half right to reach the steep edge **C** overlooking Addacomb Hole. The view, below Scar Crag on Crag Hill, to Sail and onward to Causey Pike, is both sudden and exciting, a complete terrain contrast to the springy turf that led up to the edge.

Follow the rim above Addacomb Hole to reach Wandope **D**, the summit of which is marked by a cairn. More cairns to the west and south-west mark the line of descent around the head of Third Gill. Be sure, however, to avoid the deceiving start onto Wandope's south-west ridge; go west first from the summit, until you can see the cairn at the top of Whiteless Edge.

Whiteless Edge is a narrow and exhilarating ridge with a few brief moments of exposure as it plunges down to Saddle Gate **E** before an abrupt little pull to the top of Whiteless Pike. Beyond, the path now descends steeply to Whiteless Breast, and presses on, just as steeply, to the col linking with Rannerdale Knotts.

From the col, there is a speedy way down through the secret valley of Rannerdale. But by climbing a little instead you gain the long and delightful Rannerdale ridge, passing first along Low Bank before reaching the highest point, Rannerdale Knotts. Go a little farther in a northward direction before being diverted left by steep crags for a final downward lunge to reach the valley road near Hause Point, from where the starting point is easily reached.

Rannerdale Beautiful as it is, especially in springtime when the valley is washed with the vibrant colour of bluebells, the dale has a darker side. Known also as the 'Secret Valley', this is the site of a battle at which native Cumbrians, led by Earl Boethar, routed an army of Norman soldiers under the command of Ranulph les Meschines, the Earl of Carlisle. The invaders were drawn into the confines of Rannerdale, where they were ambushed. The bluebells, so folklore says, sprang from the blood of the Norman warriors. Whether the story is true or false is irrelevant, but it formed the theme of an historical novel by local publican Nicholas Size, published in 1930 entitled *The Secret Valley*.

**9 Red Pike, High Stile and High Crag**

7½ miles (12km)

2,920 feet (890m)

**10 Pillar, Red Pike and Yewbarrow**

10 miles (16km)

4,725 feet (1,440m)

**11 Scafell Pike**

8½ miles (13.5km)

3,280 feet (1,000m)

**12 Great Gable**

6¼ miles (10km)

2,525 feet (770m)

**13 Base Brown, Green Gable, Brandreth and Grey Knotts**

8¾ miles (14km)

2,790 feet (850m)

Sour Milk Gill lower waterfall

# Western Lakeland

The fells of western Lakeland are among the highest, embracing Scafell Pike, Great Gable and Pillar, magnificent mountains, worthy of the name and splendid fare for fell wanderers. Being very much at the heart of things, these mountains can be approached from a number of directions – Borrowdale, Buttermere and Wasdale being the key valleys. And while Scafell Pike may be England's highest peak, neighbouring Scafell is one of its most difficult to access, an aspect made all the more difficult by rock falls that have, for the moment at least, pushed it from the pages of this book for safety reasons.

But Great Gable, the fell that features in the centre of the Lake District National Park's emblem, has no such deterrent, just a regal majesty squat squarely at the head both of Wasdale and Ennerdale.

Around its base prehistoric man would have travelled, carrying handiwork from their axe factories in Langdale to the coast.

In terms of British rock climbing, Wasdale and its inn, was the epicentre from which intrepid young men set out to take on the seemingly impossible crags that surrounded them. The age of mountain exploration was born here, in the cradle of Wasdale, and from it men set out to conquer the mountains of the world.

Less exalted, but no less inviting, the ridge of fells sandwiched between Buttermere and Ennerdale are an inspiration, presenting the walker with challenges to heart and lungs, and memories they will never forget.

Upper Gillercomb and Base Brown

**Start**

Buttermere

**Distance**

7½ miles (12km)

**Height gain**

2,920 feet (890m)

**Route terrain**

Rough fell walking,
craggy outcrops, steep
scree ascent and
descent; *difficult in
winter conditions*

**P** **Parking**

National Park car park
in Buttermere (Pay and
Display)

**OS maps**

Explorer OL4 (English
Lakes – North-western
area)

**GPS waypoints**

NY 173 169
🅐 NY 172 162
🅑 NY 170 148
🅒 NY 189 133
🅓 NY 187 149

# Red Pike, High Stile and High Crag

*Ranged along the south-western flanks of Buttermere, the High Stile ridge throws down a challenge that is regularly accepted by the fell walking fraternity; it is a popular and airy traverse protected from casual acquaintance by steep scree slopes at the start and more especially towards the end. Only the determined and the fit make it onto the ridge, which, in comparison, is a straightforward and hugely fulfilling romp offering striking views of the Pillar group, the two Scafells, along with Great and Green Gable on the one hand, and the Dalehead–Hindscarth–Robinson ridge on the other.*

The day begins from the car park, turning right around the **Fish Hotel** onto an enclosed track that guides you to the lakeshore (ignore the turning for Scale Force). Immediately you see what lies in store. The fells rise in extravagant fashion above the lake of Buttermere, presenting a long, dark craggy wall shaped by volcanoes into a landscape from which glaciers have subsequently gouged Bleaberry Comb and Burtness Comb.

At the lakeshore, continue along the path that leads to a footbridge spanning Buttermere Dubs and another across Sourmilk Gill, which sends its water into Buttermere lake, only for it to be immediately turned round and sent northwards into Crummock Water.

Beyond the gill, pass through a gate 🅐 into woodland and immediately engage a long flight of steps rising energetically at an angle through Burtness Wood; ignore other diverting paths. The ascent through this pleasant mixed woodland, especially agreeable on a warm day, seems longer than it is, but finally

*Red Pike from Bleaberry Tarn*

Holme Islands  Long How  FB  Reservoir
Nether How  P
Craig Houses Hotel  Buttermere
Scales  P  9  Wilkinsyke Farm
Scale Bridge  Bowderbeck
Pike Rigg  Long Crag  High Bank  Goat Crag
Low Snockrigg  High Snockrigg  Cairn 526  But
FB  A  134
Dodd  Cairns 641  Old Burtness  Burtness Wood  16  Buttermere  Dalegarth  Kirk Close
The Saddle  Pile of Stones  17  18  FB  Hassness Crag Wood  Muddoc Crags  19
Bleaberry Tarn  Horse Close
ed Pike  Chapel Crags  Waterfalls  15  D  Peggy's Bridge (FB)  102
BP  High Stile  B  Cairn  Fords
Standing Stone  BPs  Cairn  Grey Crag  Low Crag
BP  Burtness Comb  High Crag Buttress
Eagle Crag  Buttermere Fell  Warnscale
ors  Comb Crags  Sheepbone Buttress  High Wax Knott  Low Wax Knott
Raven Crag  White Cove  High Crag  14
Path  744  Gamlin End  Scarth Gap Pass
Marble Stone  CP Crags  Cairn  Scarth Gap
Seat  561  BPs  C  BP
13  Dub's Quarry (disused)

SCALE 1:26,316 OR 2½ INCHES TO 1 MILE 3.8CM TO 1KM

0  200  400  600  800 METRES  1 KILOMETRE
0  200  400  600 YARDS  ½  MILES

emerges alongside a fence, crossed at a gate.

Now a continuing, constructed, path takes over and hauls you gradually upwards, with ever improving views of the Grasmoor group of fells, and up the Buttermere valley to Fleetwith Pike. As the gradient eases a little, the path strikes westwards to run beside Sourmilk Gill, upwards to the great hollow that houses Bleaberry Tarn, a welcome and appealing place for a breather. To the south, Chapel Crags and the upper slopes of High Crag dominate, but it is the cone of Red Pike that is calling; that, and the minor outlier, Dodd.

Cross through a wall near the tarn and take to the lower, constructed part of the onward path, *which halfway up offers a branching path to anyone wanting to visit Dodd, an extension that will reward with fine views along the length of Crummock Water.*

High Stile from High Crag

As you ascend, so the constructed path gives way to scree runnels, which call for the careful placement of feet and a relaxed gait. The whole of the remaining ascent is shaly, well-worn and *potentially intimidating in high winds or icy conditions. Any winter ascent to this ridge demands the use of an ice axe and probably crampons, too.*

The summit cairn and shelter comes as a surprise and welcome relief; if the top is crowded there are numerous rocky outcrops not far away that offer shelter from most winds. The views embrace the Isle of Man and the distant Mull of Galloway.

From Red Pike start off southwards and then south-east along the rim of the cove housing Bleaberry Tarn. A line of rusted fence stanchions now serves as a guide for much of the remaining ridge. First comes a short pull onto a rocky upthrust that bears a large cairn. But this is not the summit of High Stile, which lies a little way to the north-east and calls for a slight diversion **B**.

Return to the original ridge line, and, as you progress, take in the spectacular retrospective views of High Stile's crags. Now also pressing their attentions are the great fells of the Pillar group, the Gables and, between them, Scafell Pike, looking significantly lower than neighbouring Scafell.

Onward the rusted fenceline leads you along an undulating ridge up onto High Crag, from where the descent to Scarth Gap begins abruptly. *The initial part of the descent, known as Gamlin End, is loose scree at a steep angle and is the most difficult part of the whole walk, calling for great care and focus; this is no place to stop and admire the views.* There are a number of possible lines, none significantly better than the others; the choice is yours, although one line (that on the Ennerdale side) does offer more descent on grass before being channelled into the scree.

Once the lower section is reached a clear, paved path appears, and this guides you across a minor summit, Seat, before heading down to the large cairn that marks Scarth Gap **C**.

At Scarth Gap, turn left (north-west) and follow a pleasant, steadily descending path down to the southern edge of Buttermere Lake **D**. Now all that remains is to enjoy the fine walk along the lakeshore to rejoin your outward route at the foot of Sourmilk Gill.

# Pillar, Red Pike and Yewbarrow

*This circuit of Wasdale fells is a major undertaking, a classic walk, energetic and at its best on a clear day. The advantage of starting at Overbeck is that you get the chance to warm up along the road (2 miles) before you reach Mosedale.*

### Wasdale Head Inn

Widely recognised as the cradle of British rock climbing, the Wasdale Head Inn has a long pedigree, having been used by farmers, miners, merchants and smugglers making use of the Black Sail and Sty Head mountain passes.

The first and the most famous landlord was Will Ritson, a huntsman, wrestler, farmer, fellsman, guide, raconteur, renowned as the 'The World's Biggest Liar'. Each year in nearby Santon Bridge, there is still a competition to be crowned the 'World's Biggest Liar'.

Begin with an easy stroll along the road towards **Wasdale Head Inn**. Once you reach the Wasdale Head Inn head for the Black Sail Pass, following a signed route **A** up the eastern side of Mosedale. The way is not especially difficult, dropping a little as it passes Ritson's Force, before climbing more earnestly, half-right, as you start up Gatherstone Beck.

The setting at Black Sail Pass **B** is superb with the vast gulf of Ennerdale falling away before you and then rising steeply to the High Stile ridge above Buttermere. After pausing to take in this view, continue in a north-westwards direction, towards Looking Stead, a minor summit with a grandstand view over the northern face of Pillar and Ennerdale. The path passes below Looking Stead, but it is worth making the slight diversion to its neat summit. The on-going path to Pillar rises in a series of grassy and rocky steps, a splendid line with striking views virtually every step of the way.

The summit of Pillar is rather bald, the highest point identified by a trig point and shelter cairn. From near the northern edge of the summit plateau there is a sensational view down to Pillar Rock, which spires upwards from a broad base of rock and scree.

An easy descent now leads down to Wind Gap before climbing to the bouldery unnamed summit at the top of Black Crag. Press on above Mirk Cove and follow a wall to the top of Scoat Fell **C**. This elongated fell is divided into Little Scoat Fell

## Start
Wasdale (Overbeck Bridge)

## Distance
10 miles (16km)

## Height gain
4,725 feet (1,440m)

## Route terrain
Rugged mountain paths; long and sometimes steep ascents and descents

## P Parking
Overbeck Bridge

## OS maps
Explorers OL4 (English Lakes – North-western area) and OL6 (English Lakes – South-western area)

## GPS waypoints
- NY 168 068
- **A** NY 187 090
- **B** NY 191 114
- **C** NY 159 113
- **D** NY 174 096

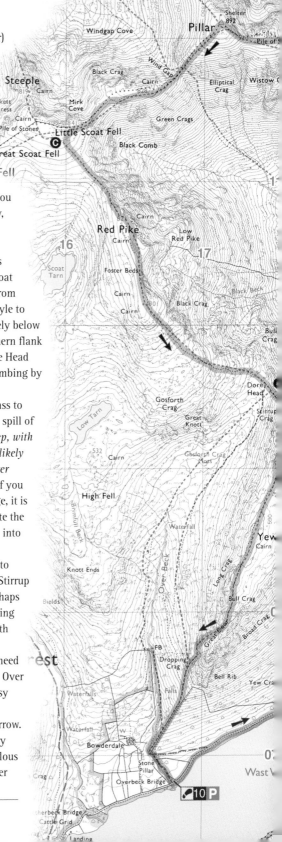

(reached first, and higher) and Great Scoat Fell, which is not visited on this walk, 'Great' here referring to bulk rather than height. Between the two a spur branches off to descend quickly to a col linking Steeple. If you have the time and energy, take in Steeple, too, it's a lovely neat summit.

A good path now leads south-east from Little Scoat Fell onto Red Pike, and from there continues in airy style to Dore Head **D**, immediately below Stirrup Crag on the northern flank of Yewbarrow. From Dore Head you can avoid further climbing by descending directly into Mosedale, keeping on grass to the left of a badly eroded spill of scree. *This descent is steep, with a sense of exposure, and likely to be troublesome in winter conditions or after rain.* If you started at Overbeck Bridge, it is almost as easy to complete the walk rather than descend into Mosedale.

To continue, you need to attack the severe face of Stirrup Crag, through which, perhaps surprisingly, an entertaining way is found. Walkers with no taste for such craggy confrontation, however, need only move right, towards Over Beck, to find a steep grassy slope offering an easier, slanting line onto Yewbarrow.

Continue across the airy top of Yewbarrow, a fabulous striding summit with super

views, although in late July and August a diversion to the bilberry-laden slopes overlooking Wasdale will prove tasty, and may delay you.

As the ridge starts to drop, a good path leads you down through Dropping Crag and Bell Rib to Overbeck Bridge. This descent requires care and can be slippery in almost all conditions. *A winter descent may prove awkward, and require the use of crampons.*

SCALE 1:26316 or 2½ INCHES to 1 MILE 3.8CM to 1KM

| 0 | 200 | 400 | 600 | 800 METRES 1 |
|---|-----|-----|-----|--------------|

KILOMETRES
MILES

| 0 | 200 | 400 | 600 YARDS | ½ |
|---|-----|-----|-----------|---|

*Looking Stead and Pillar, with Pillar Rock (right)*

# Scafell Pike

### Start
Seathwaite

### Distance
8½ miles (13.5km)

### Height gain
3,280 feet (1,000m)

### Route terrain
Rough fell walking, craggy outcrops, loose scree and rocks

### Parking
Limited roadside parking along the lane to Seathwaite Farm

### OS maps
Explorers OL4 (English Lakes – North-western area) and OL6 (English Lakes – South-western area)

### GPS waypoints
NY 235 122
Ⓐ NY 229 109
Ⓑ NY 219 095
Ⓒ NY 222 094
Ⓓ NY 211 076
Ⓔ NY 227 080
Ⓕ NY 232 081
Ⓖ NY 229 087

*Scafell Pike succeeds in pulling the crowds on mere altitude alone. The fell's attractions are many, but most are available only to those who approach on foot. So, to really enjoy the ascent of England's highest peak, this walk from Seathwaite uses two classic lines to produce a synergy of experiences that prove beyond doubt that two-plus-two definitely makes five.*

From Seathwaite there is no clue as to the whereabouts of Scafell Pike, but what is visible is the long, rising valley to the south, occupied by the bullying watercourse of Grains Gill. This is the route used on the descent, and its line is crossed at the single-arched Stockley Bridge. There is a broad, stony track all the way to Stockley Bridge, but a more pleasurable start begins through an archway at Seathwaite Farm beyond which a path leads to a footbridge spanning the infant River Derwent.

Once over the bridge, turn left through a gate and take a clear path across the lower slopes of Base Brown until the path swings upwards into the ravine that houses Taylorgill Force Ⓐ. The waterfall is a lovely mare's tail; the path to its right an interesting exercise in easy rock work leading to a surprise gate, and beyond.

Once free of the ravine, the gradient eases considerably as a stony path leads on to Styhead Tarn, perfectly set between Seathwaite Fell and the Gables, Great and Green. The tarn sits along the route of a long-established thoroughfare linking Borrowdale and Wasdale, a dalesman's route. Crossing this watershed in the opposite direction, from the direction of Langdale into Ennerdale, runs the course of a route taken by the prehistoric axe makers of Langdale, bound for the western coast.

Only at Styhead Ⓑ does Scafell Pike finally condescend to put in an appearance, and still seems far away. The multiplicity of routes here requires a moment's careful navigation if you are not to wander off down the Wasdale track, or up to Esk Hause. The surest line, however, does set off along the Esk Hause route, briefly in an eastwards direction, but soon you encounter a couple of paths branching on the right Ⓒ, now heading south. The second path is the drier of the two. *This line of ascent is known as the Corridor Route, a superb traverse, but a long and rough line on which care*

Ling

Hollow Stones

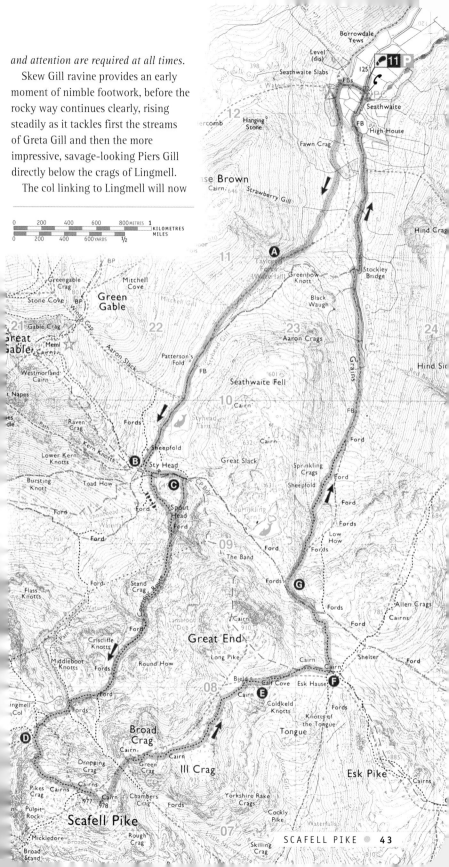

*and attention are required at all times.*

Skew Gill ravine provides an early moment of nimble footwork, before the rocky way continues clearly, rising steadily as it tackles first the streams of Greta Gill and then the more impressive, savage-looking Piers Gill directly below the crags of Lingmell.

The col linking to Lingmell will now

start to drop away to your right, although strong walkers would have no difficulty diverting that way and adding the seldom-visited summit to the day's tally. The main path rises above the col and meets with a path **D** ascending via Hollow Stones. Now all that remains is to plod the rocky path to the summit of the fell.

The way down is no less spectacular, and offers the opportunity for brief diversions to take in adjacent fells that are rarely visited. But the start of the return descent begins in a north-easterly direction, down a badly eroded ridge to the narrow col linking Scafell Pike and Broad Crag. Beyond the col lies a mass of boulders; this is Broad Crag. A path does contrive to find a way through, over and around the boulders, but the adventurous and sure-footed will find pleasure in bouldering up to the top of Broad Crag.

Another col links Broad Crag and Ill Crag to the east. The path crosses the col, but so few walkers ever bother to turn aside to take in Ill Crag, a lonely outpost above Little Narrowcove, high above the headwaters of Great Moss.

A second bouldery episode lies to the north of Ill Crag, but nothing like as awkward as Broad Crag. Once beyond

this, the path swings half-right into a little hollow known as Calf Cove **E**. *On a clear day, it is easy to wander up onto the top of Great End, bringing this summit, too, into the day. But then return to Calf Cove.*

As you descend Calf Cove, so a broad track slips down to the massive pass known as Esk Hause, but before reaching the lowest point you can branch left (northwards) on a rough path **F** that runs down to intercept the path from Styhead to Esk Hause.

Grains Gill lies ahead, the upper part known as Ruddy Gill for reasons that are apparent when you reach it **G**. Here you abandon the Styhead path, cross Ruddy Gill and immediately join a good restored path parallel with the ravine (on your left), following the course of Ruddy Gill. It is a splendid descent; on your left are the slopes of Seathwaite Fell, while on the right those of the long whaleback of Allen Crags and Glaramara.

It seems to take an eternity to make the descent, but eventually you arrive alongside a wall running to a gate through which lies Stockley Bridge. Once over the bridge, a broad, stony track now leads directly back to Seathwaite Farm, which does a popular trade in light refreshments.

*Scafell Pike from Crinkle Crags*

# Great Gable

**Start**

Seathwaite

**Distance**

6¼ miles (10km)

**Height gain**

2,525 feet (770m)

**Route terrain**

Rough fell walking, craggy outcrops, scree; *difficult in winter conditions*

**Parking**

Limited roadside parking along the lane to Seathwaite Farm

**OS maps**

Explorer OL4 (English Lakes – North-western area)

**GPS waypoints**

🖉 NY 235 122
Ⓐ NY 229 109
Ⓑ NY 219 095
Ⓒ NY 214 105

*Great Gable enjoys arguably the most iconic of Lakeland profiles, featuring as it does in the National Park's emblem. This is a summit that symbolises the spirit of fell walking in the Lakes, the one fell that everyone comes to conquer sooner or later, the quintessential Lakeland fell. There are numerous ways to its summit and some, as with the present route, are generally straightforward.*

🖉 At Seathwaite Farm, a gap in the buildings gives onto a walled path that leads to a footbridge spanning the River Derwent. Once over the bridge, turn left through a gate, and follow a developing path rising steadily above the river as it crosses and then rounds the skirts of Base Brown.

Ahead lie Aaron Crags at the northern end of Seathwaite Fell, to the left the huge bulk of Glaramara. But your attention is soon drawn to the mare's-tail splash of Taylorgill Force Ⓐ, where Styhead Gill plunges over the lip of the modest hanging valley that runs south-westwards to Styhead Tarn. The path keeps to the north of the waterfall, still clinging to the lower slopes of Base Brown, and requiring a hands-on approach in a few places.

Eventually, the path climbs above the falls, and pitches into a rather vague terrain, rarely dry, but neither excessively wet. The gill serves as a guide, leading onwards for some distance and across the base of Aaron Slack, a prominent scree route on the right by which route we return. Pass the lovely Styhead Tarn, a jewel set against the backdrop of Great End, with Broad Crag and distant Scafell Pike forming a framework ahead. Press on to a prominent path junction Ⓑ, which also serves as a convenient and sensible resting point before you begin the climb onto Great Gable.

From this point paths go in all directions, so it is worth a moment to locate that rising onto the slopes of Great Gable. From this angle, the fell has no appealing outline, little to draw you on. But all that soon changes. As for the paths, take one too far to the west and you start heading down into Wasdale. Not far enough to the north west and you find yourself on a precarious route bound for Kern Knotts and Napes Needle. You should be going upwards in a north-westerly direction,

*Approaching Styhead*

pursuing a route that has undergone much improvement in recent years, and is now much more accommodating than the scree and loose rock of old.

How long you take to reach the summit is up to you, but frequent pauses will only enhance the experience as Wasdale and the Scafells come more clearly into view. When you get there, the summit is a confusing array of boulders, but a place of national importance, given to the National Trust in 1923 by the Fell and Rock Climbing Club as a memorial to its members killed in the First World War; each year a service of remembrance is held on the summit.

A little away from the main summit stands the Westmorland Cairn, located about 150yds south west of the summit.

*There are two ways to go from the summit; one is to retrace your steps to Styhead, the other, the preferred route, but one that requires great care, heads roughly in a north-easterly direction, towards Green Gable. Take time to locate the route with confidence if visibility is not good.*

The way leads down to Windy Gap **⊙**, so named for reasons that will become obvious on all but the balmiest of days. Once on the narrow col, turn right and heads downwards in a south-easterly direction, following a long, neat ravine known as Aaron Slack.

*Aaron Slack begins as a slithery, loose scree and rock descent: tread carefully.* Lower down a pitched path appears, offering more secure footing. Then, given that there is no lake up above, you are joined by what is a surprising amount of water in the form of a busy stream. Keep following the widening ravine downwards until you rejoin your outward route near Styhead Tarn.

Turn left (north east), and follow the popular path out towards the upper Seathwaite valley. When you reach a wooden footbridge, cross it, and continue on the other side, which offers a variant to the route you took up alongside Taylorgill Force. The on-going path is secure enough, and leads steadily down to a wall, and then down some more to Stockley Bridge. Now all that remains is to cross the bridge and follow the broad track back to Seathwaite Farm.

*Variant finish:*
*From the top of Aaron Slack there is a fine variant finish that begins with a little more uphill work, but is then all downhill. This climbs by a loose scree slope onto the summit of Green Gable, from where a path sets off initially northwards, but then quite soon branching right and descending towards the head of Gillercomb. After an initial bout of dancing through low rock outcrops, the path slips down to the grassy col linking Green Gable with Base Brown. From the col, a path turns left and zigzags down into Gillercomb, a splendid hanging valley. Once the first stage of the descent is complete, a more*

*or less level path runs on across the northern slopes of Base Brown to the very lip of the valley. Descend more steeply to a gate in a wall from where a clear path now plunges down to the Seathwaite Valley below, requiring hands for security in a few places as*

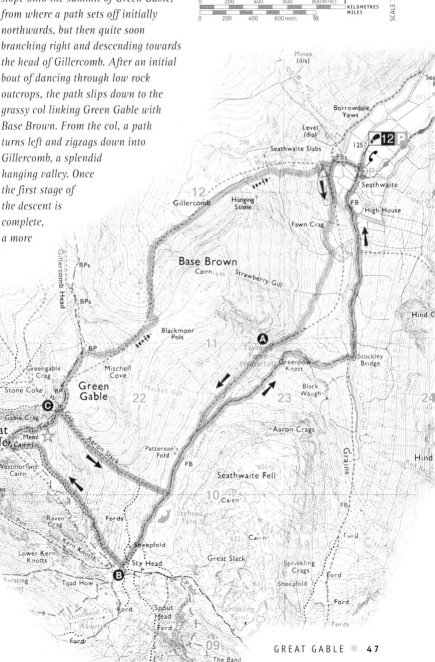

*you pass over glaciated rock bands, and for the most part in the company of Sour Milk Gill and its cascades. Towards the foot of the descent, an awkward ladder-stile crosses a wall not far from the Derwent bridge used at the* start of the walk. All that remains is to stroll out to Seathwaite Farm.

Using this variant shortens the overall distance to 5½ miles (8.75km), but increases the height gain to 2,660 feet (810m).

Great Gable from Green Gable

# Base Brown, Green Gable, Brandreth and Grey Knotts

walk 13

**Start**

Seatoller

**Distance**

8¾ miles (14km)

**Height gain**

2,790 feet (850m)

**Route terrain**

Rough fell walking, craggy outcrops, scree, some road walking

**Parking**

Car park (Pay and Display)

**OS maps**

Explorer OL4 (English Lakes – North-western area)

**GPS waypoints**

  NY 245 138
Ⓐ NY 250 137
Ⓑ NY 228 121
Ⓒ NY 222 111
Ⓓ NY 215 127
Ⓔ NY 233 137

*Many walkers who visit Green Gable then go on to tackle the final steep pull onto neighbouring Great Gable, which is a perfectly valid enterprise. But doing so means that other summits, worthy of our attention, are passed by. So, this circuit modifies the Great Gable plan, by omitting it altogether (but it is visited in Walk 12), and opting for a grand circular tour that makes the most of the Seathwaite arm of Borrowdale, and includes a visit to the slate mines at Honister.*

Just by Strands Bridge Ⓐ on the Borrowdale–Honister road, a wide track, part of the Allerdale Ramble, sets off southwards into the Seathwaite branch of the valley. The bridge can be reached either by simply walking down the road from the Seatoller car park (600 yds), or by the rather safer expedient of a footpath leaving the rear of the car park bound for Longthwaite youth hostel and Rosthwaite. After 500 yds, you can leave this path and head for Folly Bridge, spanning the River Derwent, and from there walking out to reach the road close by Strands Bridge.

Once on the track, simply take pleasure in following it past Thorneythwaite Farm and on finally to reach the farm buildings and cottages at Seathwaite. In the middle of the cluster, a footpath sets off through the buildings, heading for the Derwent and the conspicuous white gash of Sour Milk Gill. You

**Hanging valleys**   A hanging valley is a tributary or side valley with its base at a higher level than the main valley into which it flows. They are associated with U-shaped valleys, like Seathwaite, when a tributary glacier flows into a glacier of larger volume. The main glacier erodes a deep U-shaped valley with steep sides while the tributary glacier, having a smaller volume of ice and therefore less force, creates a shallower U-shaped valley. Since the surfaces of the glaciers were originally at the same elevation, the shallower valley appears to be 'hanging' above the main valley, a circumstance that often creates telltale waterfalls to form at or near the outlet of the upper valley.

cross the Derwent by a gated footbridge, and then continue directly ahead to an awkwardly angled ladder-stile crossing a wall. Once over this test of balance, you gain a good path, pitched in parts, that winds upwards, and brings you to a fine vantage point close by the gill's lower waterfall.

Onward and upward you may need to use your hands to aid balance as you clamber through a rocky section, but then an easy path takes you up to a gate in a wall, beyond which a little more climbing leads you past the upper falls and up to the lip of the hanging valley of Gillercomb, overlooked by Base Brown on your left and Raven Crag (on Grey Knotts) to your right. This is a magnificent location, and as the gradient levels you can make out the limits of what would once have been a shallow glacial lake backed by an extensive rash of moraines, or drumlins.

As you enter Gillercomb **B**, so the path levels for a while, taking you towards the head of the valley where it starts to climb again, finishing in a zigzag flourish that places you on the broad ridge **C** linking Green Gable and Base Brown. *To visit Base Brown, simply turn left and follow a clear path to the large cairn that marks its summit.* Then retrace your steps, and follow a stony path up to the top of Green Gable, just before which the path is joined by that coming in from the right, from the direction of Brandreth.

The beauty of this approach to Green Gable is that you get no forewarning of the stunning views awaiting you. Most obvious, of course, are the crags of Great Gable, but if you take a moment to orientate yourself and spin slowly in

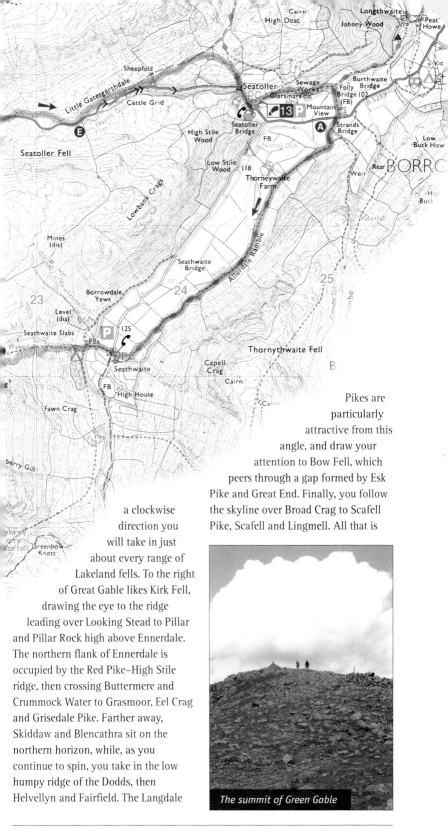

Pikes are particularly attractive from this angle, and draw your attention to Bow Fell, which peers through a gap formed by Esk Pike and Great End. Finally, you follow the skyline over Broad Crag to Scafell Pike, Scafell and Lingmell. All that is a clockwise direction you will take in just about every range of Lakeland fells. To the right of Great Gable likes Kirk Fell, drawing the eye to the ridge leading over Looking Stead to Pillar and Pillar Rock high above Ennerdale. The northern flank of Ennerdale is occupied by the Red Pike–High Stile ridge, then crossing Buttermere and Crummock Water to Grasmoor, Eel Crag and Grisedale Pike. Farther away, Skiddaw and Blencathra sit on the northern horizon, while, as you continue to spin, you take in the low humpy ridge of the Dodds, then Helvellyn and Fairfield. The Langdale

*The summit of Green Gable*

missing from this spectacular panorama is the view down into Wasdale, and for that you need to visit Great Gable – but not today, perhaps.

The top of Green Gable is marked by a large cairn and two stone shelters, with lines of cairns leading southwards to Windy Gap, and northwards, back the way you have come. Follow this latter route, but then branch left rather than back into Gillercomb, and follow a clear path and a few rusting fence stanchions, that take you across Gillercomb Head and up onto Brandreth, and then easily across the rocky interlude to Grey Knotts.

There is a direct and steep path from Grey Knotts down to Honister Hause, but an easier option simply strikes westwards over rough ground until you intercept a clear path **D**, known as Moses' Trod (named after Moses Rigg, an illicit whisky distiller, quarryman, rogue and general ne'r do well), that now runs northwards to meet the path ascending from Honister. Now turn right (east) and descend to the slate works and the road at the top of the Honister Path.

The final stage of the walk, between Honister and Seatoller sets off by following the road, but some of the road

## Honister Quarry

Quarrying at Honister has probably been undertaken since Roman times, although contemporary records have nothing to say until the early 1700s. These days you can make guided visitor trips to the mines, but for the early workers, conditions were harsh and dangerous. Slate was brought down to the knapping sheds on hurdles or trail barrows, which had two inclined handles, known as stangs, at the front between which the man would position himself to haul the load. These contraptions weighed anything up to 80 pounds, and it took the men half an hour to carry them back up to the quarry, although the laden descent was only a matter of minutes. Some of the tales surrounding this form of work are remarkable: Samuel Trimmer once made 15 journeys in a day for a bottle of rum and a small percentage of the slate he brought down. Joseph Clarke of Stonethwaite made 17 journeys in one day, bringing down 640 pounds of slate each time, a total of almost 11,000 pounds.

walking can be avoided by old tracks on the left as you descend, and then when a longer track branches left **E** you can follow it all the way down to the Seatoller car park, away from the busy road.

Gillercomb

**South and Central Lakeland**

Dow Crag and Buck
Pike from Torver Bridge

# South and Central Lakeland

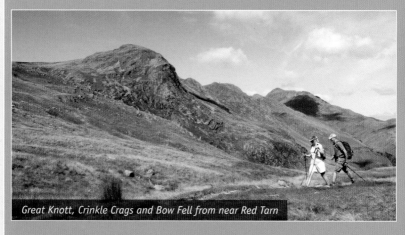

*Great Knott, Crinkle Crags and Bow Fell from near Red Tarn*

So easily accessible from the central road network at Ambleside, Greater and, for that matter, Little Langdale are hugely popular. It is a quality enhanced by the great ring of mountains – Harrison Stickle, Bow Fell, Crinkle Crags and Pike o'Blisco – that lie at the head of the dale, a formidable barrier to westerly progress. Fortunately, there is more than enough in Langdale to keep visitors occupied whether intent on the tops or satisfied with delightful woodland wandering in the valleys.

To the south rise the fells on Coniston, introduced by the heights of Swirl How and Grey Friar, and Wetherlam, an isolated summit overlooking the enclave of Tilberthwaite. But everyone is drawn to Coniston, the lake, the village and the mountain. Here, in the shadow of the Old Man, Lakeland industry is more evident than elsewhere, but detracts little from the overall scene of cragginess and mist-dusted tops. What, in particular, it is about The Old Man of Coniston that draws the crowds is difficult to say; it is not the most striking of summits, nor is it approached, other than from the west, by a route that holds its own intrigue. Yet popular it remains. So those in search of away-from-it-all-ness will need to press on from the Old Man, to the spectacular ridge that tops the cliffs of Dow Crag and descends slowly to the ancient thoroughfare of the Walna Scar Road. Now you can hear yourself think, and snuggle among rocks in the companionship of silence and solitude.

# Crinkle Crags and Bow Fell

walk  14

*The sight of the crenellated Crinkle Crags at the head of Oxendale is both daunting and compelling, a splendid challenge to every fell walker. Here the ascent is combined with that of adjacent Bow Fell to give a fair old day's walking, but with the advantage that you can opt out before tackling Bow Fell, and descend via The Band.*

Set off from the car park at Old Dungeon Ghyll, and as the lane turns out to the valley road, go ahead through a gate and onto a brief path leading to a single arch bridge spanning Great Langdale Beck. Over the bridge, go forward to meet the road, but immediately turn right onto a surfaced access road to Stool End Farm, a splendid stretch along which to warm up muscles and take in the great cirque of mountains that surrounds you. The way through the farmyard is waymarked, and finally keeps left to a gate giving onto a stony track rising beside a wall.

When the track divides **Ⓐ**, keep left, descending gently into Oxendale, through a gate and on as far as a sheepfold. Once past this, with Oxendale Beck on your left, you soon reach a footbridge, with the onward path racing up the fellside beyond. Just over the bridge the next 100 yds is more or less level, but is the last level ground you will meet for some considerable time; make the most of it.

At a cairn **Ⓑ** you begin the long, steep pull upwards to round the rocky knoll of Brown Howe. Much of the path is pitched, and the going is not quite so bad as it seems from below, Throughout the climb, the toil is tempered by ever-improving views of Bow Fell rising above the conspicuous ravine of Hell Gill, and of Crinkle Crags.

Once above Brown Howe, a spectacular vision appears; that of the deeply incised ravine of Browney Gill, a quite superb gash that gathers waters from Red Tarn above. Briefly the gradient levels, but then only steady uphill work remains until you arrive at a path T-junction **Ⓒ**, where you intercept the path from the Three Shire Stone near the top of the Wrynose Pass.

Turn right onto a rising path that soon brings Red Tarn retrospectively into view, and climbs steadily with the knobbly summit of Cold Pike on your left and Great Knott on the right;

## Sidebar

### Start
Langdale valley (Old Dungeon Ghyll)

### Distance
9¼ miles (15km)

### Height gain
3,610 feet (1,100m)

### Route terrain
Rough fell walking, craggy outcrops, scree, a little (avoidable) scrambling

### Parking
National Trust car park (Pay and Display)

### OS maps
Explorer OL6 (English Lakes – South-western area)

### GPS waypoints
- NY 286 061
- Ⓐ NY 275 056
- Ⓑ NY 270 052
- Ⓒ NY 267 039
- Ⓓ NY 248 060
- Ⓔ NY 240 072
- Ⓕ NY 247 075
- Ⓖ NY 261 073

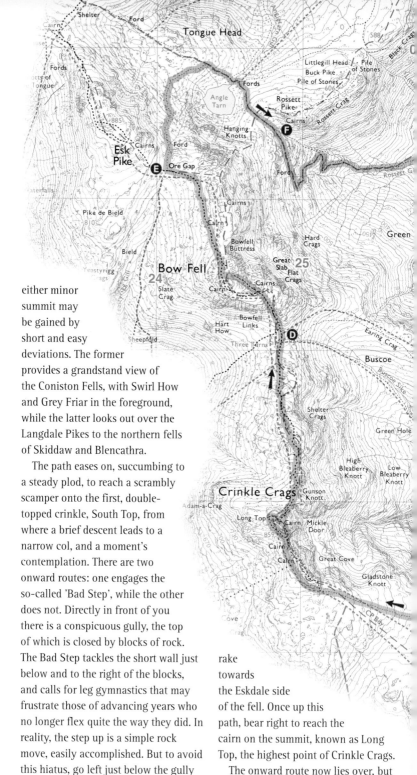

either minor summit may be gained by short and easy deviations. The former provides a grandstand view of the Coniston Fells, with Swirl How and Grey Friar in the foreground, while the latter looks out over the Langdale Pikes to the northern fells of Skiddaw and Blencathra.

The path eases on, succumbing to a steady plod, to reach a scrambly scamper onto the first, double-topped crinkle, South Top, from where a brief descent leads to a narrow col, and a moment's contemplation. There are two onward routes: one engages the so-called 'Bad Step', while the other does not. Directly in front of you there is a conspicuous gully, the top of which is closed by blocks of rock. The Bad Step tackles the short wall just below and to the right of the blocks, and calls for leg gymnastics that may frustrate those of advancing years who no longer flex quite the way they did. In reality, the step up is a simple rock move, easily accomplished. But to avoid this hiatus, go left just below the gully to reach a clear path ascending a grassy rake towards the Eskdale side of the fell. Once up this path, bear right to reach the cairn on the summit, known as Long Top, the highest point of Crinkle Crags.

The onward route now lies over, but mostly around, the next three crinkles,

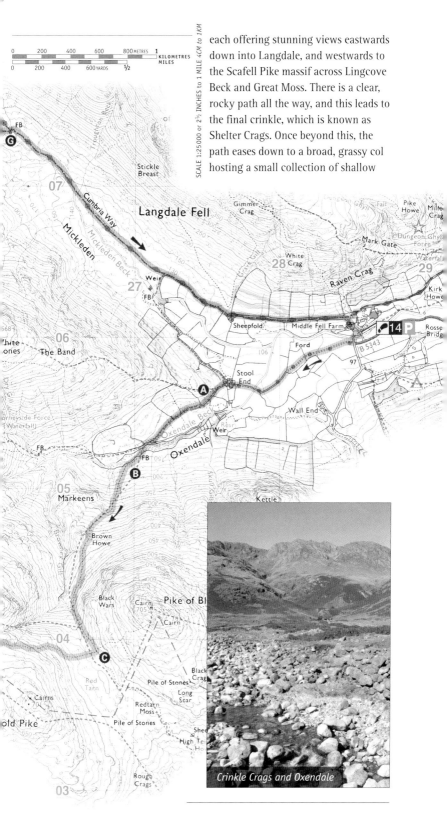

each offering stunning views eastwards down into Langdale, and westwards to the Scafell Pike massif across Lingcove Beck and Great Moss. There is a clear, rocky path all the way, and this leads to the final crinkle, which is known as Shelter Crags. Once beyond this, the path eases down to a broad, grassy col hosting a small collection of shallow

*Crinkle Crags and Oxendale*

*Climbing out of Oxendale*

ponds, known as the Three Tarns **D**. (It is from here that anyone wanting to truncate the walk, can seek out the cairned top of The Band, and follow this confidently back down to Stool End Farm.)

From Three Tarns, the continuation up Bow Fell is by a conspicuous scree slope that finishes with a final rocky flourish to the summit of the fell.

To complete the walk, leave the summit in a northerly direction taking a cairned and steadily descending route to another col, Ore Gap **E**.

From the col descend northwards beneath the crags of Esk Pike, aiming to the west of Angle Tarn, around which a path circles to gain a more substantial track below Tongue Head, an ancient, probably prehistoric, route across the fells.

From Angle Tarn the path rises a little as it heads for a gap **F** to the south of Rossett Pike. Beyond, a much-restored path plunges into the head of Mickleden, slipping downwards to meet the Cumbria Way at a wooden footbridge **G** at the foot of the Stake Pass. Now all that remains is to follow a straightforward route in a south-easterly direction back to Old Dungeon Ghyll.

# Harrison Stickle and Pike of Stickle

**walk 15**

**Start**
Great Langdale, New Dungeon Ghyll

**Distance**
6½ miles (10.5km)

**Height gain**
2,640 feet (805m)

**Route terrain**
Rough fell walking, craggy outcrops, moorland

**Parking**
Stickle Ghyll NT car park (Pay and Display)

**OS maps**
Explorer OL6 (English Lakes – South-western area)

**GPS waypoints**
🖉 NY 294 064
Ⓐ NY 288 075
Ⓑ NY 278 073
Ⓒ NY 265 087

*Harrison Stickle and Pike of Stickle have a distinctive profile and are in view from many parts of the Lake District; recognisable enough to have served as the icon for the national park had not Wasdale been favoured instead. The combination of these two fells is a straightforward up-and-down affair, but is here concluded by a cross-moorland romp to the ancient crossing point at Stake Pass before returning through the valley of Mickleden.*

🖉 Set off from the Stickle Ghyll car park in Great Langdale by taking a path to the left of the buildings at the rear of the car park and following a brief, enclosed way that leads out to a junction of paths close by Stickle Ghyll. When the path divides, keep right, beside the ghyll to locate a path leading to a bridge spanning the watercourse.

There has been much-needed path improvement work on the route up to Stickle Tarn, but it is still rough. Higher up, the path divides, but both options lead unerringly to Stickle Tarn Ⓐ set against the breathtaking cliffs of Pavey Ark. Not until the last few strides does the uphill work cease, but when it does you find yourself in a remarkable and exciting place. The tarn is serene and pleasant enough, but the eye is inevitably drawn to Pavey Ark across the face of which a diagonal line marks the course of Jack's Rake, a moderate rock climb, but something to which everyone is drawn, sooner or later. For now, it is later.

Cross the outflow of the tarn and take to the obvious path, paved in places, to the right of the buttresses on Harrison Stickle. Eventually you intercept a path arriving from the direction of Pavey Ark; when you reach it take either of two paths going left onto the rocky top of Harrison Stickle. The highest point, marked by one of many cairns, lies at the northern end of the neat summit plateau, and brings a view of great attraction. On a clear day it would be hard to find a better place from which to appreciate the landscapes of the Lake District.

To continue, the surest way is to set off initially in a northerly direction, as if heading for Thunacar Knott, but then curving to the west and south-west into the boggy hollow of Harrison Combe at the top of Dungeon Ghyll Ⓑ. There is a prominent scree path that leaves Harrison Stickle summit in a westwards direction and leads to the same patch of marshy ground, but it is easier on the legs just to give this a wide berth. To the south lies nothing but trouble.

From Harrison Combe, continue west to the base of the cone that is Pike of Stickle, on the way passing the top of a huge scree shoot cascading downwards to the valley floor. Do not be tempted this way; many are, with varying degrees of triumph. Go past this and continue to the foot of Pike of Stickle from where a largely hands-on ascent is required to raise you to yet another magnificent viewpoint overlooking Mickleden, The Band, Oxendale and Pike o'Blisco; off to the right lie Crinkle Crags and Bow Fell, and even Great Gable muscles in on the act, beyond Rossett Pike.

Now a lovely moorland romp awaits: leave Pike of Stickle by your line of ascent, and then bear left (north-west) along a path across the grassy expanse of Martcrag Moor, which on some early maps, thanks to a delightful error, was written as Martcrag Moo – so much more mysterious.

The cross-moor path eventually intercepts the Cumbria Way at the top of Stake Pass ●. Now turn left and amble down the path to the foot of Rossett Gill and the head of Mickleden from where a broad, clear path leads back to civilisation. As you approach the buildings at Old Dungeon Ghyll, keep left through a gate onto a stony track that undulates all the way back to New Dungeon Ghyll. You may notice

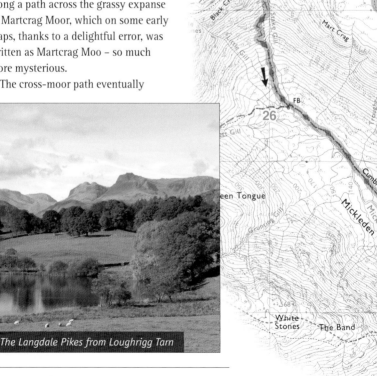

The Langdale Pikes from Loughrigg Tarn

*Harrison Stickle and Pike of Stickle from Green Gable*

that along some stretches the wall on your left, i.e. northern, flank is composed of significantly larger and more irregular boulders than that on the left. This outer wall is the original ring garth of Langdale, the boundary of the intake land, something that can be traced around the greater part of the valley – virtually an ancient monument in its own right.

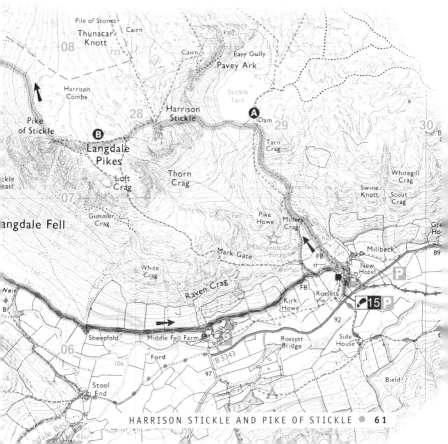

# Old Man of Coniston and Dow Crag

**Start**

Coniston

**Distance**

8½ miles (13.5km)

**Height gain**

3,100 feet (945m)

**Route terrain**

Rough fell walking, quarry spoil heaps; craggy outcrops, scree; *difficult in winter conditions*

**P Parking**

In the village (Pay and Display: cash and credit card) – see note on page 65 for alternative start/finish at the site of Coniston station

**OS maps**

Explorer OL6 (English Lakes – South-western area)

**GPS waypoints**

🖉 SD 304 975
Ⓐ SD 284 981
Ⓑ SD 275 982
Ⓒ SD 266 982
Ⓓ SD 258 965
Ⓔ SD 289 970
Ⓕ SD 290 966
Ⓖ SD 299 968

*Once the highest summit in Lancashire, a distinction it lost in 1974, the Old Man dominates the village of Coniston and is a readily identifiable landmark, albeit not an attractive one, from far afield. Most visitors content themselves with this one summit alone, but in this walk, a greater circuit is made, embracing the ridge of Dow Crag and descending to the Walna Scar road, an ancient packhorse route.*

🖉 As you leave the main car park in Coniston, turn left into the village to the main road. Cross the road-bridge spanning Church Beck, and then turn right in front of Coppermines Cottages onto a minor road that leads up to the **Sun Hotel**.

> **The Sun Inn** There has been an inn at this location since the days of the packhorse trains, quite probably previously known as the Rising Sun and dating from the 17th century, although the date over the doorway of the present hotel says 1902. The Sun Inn certainly appears as such in records from 1829. The hotel extension was added when the railway came in 1859.

Walk past the hotel, and behind it, turn right onto a signposted path for the 'Old Man and Levers Water'. Road surfacing continues briefly, but then you reach a gate beyond which a rough track leads on through Dixon Ground to cross Scrow Beck. The track now briefly enters light woodland before running on agreeably to reach the Miners Bridge at the entrance to Coppermines valley.

Do not cross the bridge, but keep ahead at this point, moving onto a narrow path and gaining height gently as you gradually pass around the northern end of a minor summit, The Bell, and then rise to meet a well-constructed track, arriving from the direction of the Walna Scar road at a bend Ⓐ. Turn right, but ignore a tempting track on the right, to follow a more substantial track as it twists upwards through increasingly rough terrain and huge spills of quarry spoil.

The on-going path is clear enough, now improved in a number of sections, and climbing steadily to reach Low Water Ⓑ, a

The Old Man of Coniston from Coniston Water

beautiful tarn reposing in an enormous cirque of cliffs and steep slopes. This is one of Lakeland's grandest settings, the hue of the water, tinted blue by copper, injecting brightness into the scene on all but the gloomiest of days. It makes an ideal place to take a breather before tackling the final pull.

The top of the Old Man lies directly above, as the crow flies a mere 550 yds distant, but with 720 feet of height gain still to acquire. To reach the summit you must follow a rough and very steep path zigzagging across the south wall of this corrie. Once at the top, turn right, and follow a broad, shaly path to the summit. The trig pillar is in a commanding position overlooking the Low Water basin.

The continuation leaves the summit in a north-westerly then westerly direction, as if heading first for Brim Fell. *In poor visibility, the line is not clear, but it descends quite steeply to a broad col* ⊙ *due north of Goat's Water. Anyone no longer feeling disposed to tackle Dow Crag, can here descend southwards to pass Goat's Water and meet up with the Walna Scar road, not far from a bridge spanning Torver Beck (SD 271 965).*

The way onto Dow Crag (pronounced 'doe') is straightforward enough, easing upwards to the rocky summit, which affords a fine view of the Old Man, albeit of his posterior.

The eastern edge of Dow Crag is defined by steep and over-hanging

**First ascent** The first recorded ascent of the Old Man of Coniston was in 1792 by Captain Joseph Budworth, who had already that day walked from Ambleside to Coniston, to see the lake, and found himself unable to resist the challenge of the fell. Sustained only by brandy, he completed the ascent, and still walked back to Ambleside.

crags, the playground of rock climbers, and this escarpment, not to be followed too closely, guides you southwards across the tops of a few yawning gullies to Buck Pike and then Brown Pike, beyond which a sudden change of direction takes the descending path in a south-westerly direction until it intercepts the Walna Scar road **D**.

Turn left and now descend this old packhorse trail, rough and ready near the top, but improving as you head down to Torver Bridge. The evident track ultimately ends at a popular parking area – used by folk who want to abbreviate the ascent of the Old Man – and from here you can pass through the nearby gate onto a surfaced lane and follow that back to Coniston.

But there is a better, safer option. As you reach the gate **E**, turn right alongside a wall, following a footpath for Bleathwaite. The path is clear, and virtually level, leading to a point where it intercepts a bridleway, a variant on the old packhorse route. Here, next to a tall ladder-stile **F**, pass through the left-hand one of two gates, going forward initially on a rough track beside a wall, but later following the sunken course of an old highway, flanked by ancient hawthorns. Ahead, there is a fine view of the middle section of Coniston Water backed by the wooded

## Coniston Branch Railway

A railway was first introduced as a narrow gauge line to Coniston to service the copper mines, but later, as a standard gauge upgrade, served passengers, opening on 18 June 1859. Unfortunately, completion of the branch line coincided with the peak period of copper mine activity, following which there was a steady decline during the 1860s, and a rather more rapid one during the 1870s. Forced to rely on tourist traffic, the Coniston branch line was at a disadvantage, as it faced in completely the wrong direction, and its terminus, originally built to service the mines, was high above the village, away from the lake that visitors came to see. Although the line remained open until 1958, it never overcame its inherent disadvantages, and closed on 6 October of that year.

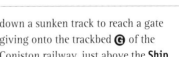

slopes of Monk Coniston Moor.

The path eventually descends into a narrow wooded dell around a stream. Here the track swings sharply to the right. After about 40 yds, the track enters a narrow walled section. Ignore this, and instead go left, through a bridlegate, to continue descending beside the stream. Lower down, you reach the first of a group of cottages at High Beck. Head down the concrete access track, but after about 100 yds leave the track by branching left with the on-going bridleway (waymark), which here runs alongside a wall and at the lower edge of a large, managed garden area, which it soon leaves at a bridle-gate.

Continue across rough pasture, through which the bridleway is waymarked, and descends once more down a sunken track to reach a gate giving onto the trackbed **G** of the Coniston railway, just above the **Ship Inn**. Turn left along the trackbed, and follow it towards Coniston to reach the edge of a small housing estate.

The site of the Coniston station is now a public car park (SD 300 974), one that serves as an alternative start for this walk.

Go past the station site and descend Old Furness Road to a T-junction, where it meets the lower end of the Walna Scar road. Turn right, and follow the road as it swings to the right, but having done so, take the first turning on the left to re-appear at the Sun Inn. Now simply retrace your steps into Coniston.

SCALE 1:25000 or 2½ INCHES to 1 MILE 4CM to 1KM

# Wetherlam

**Start**

Tilberthwaite

**Distance**

5½ miles (8.75km)

**Height gain**

2,280 feet (695m)

**Route terrain**

Rough fell walking, craggy outcrops, mine and quarry workings

**Parking**

Parking areas either side of Yewdale Beck

**OS maps**

Explorer OL6 (English Lakes – South-western area)

**GPS waypoints**

NY 306 010
Ⓐ NY 299 010
Ⓑ NY 293 016
Ⓒ SD 293 990
Ⓓ NY 299 007

*Tilberthwaite Gill was hugely popular in Victorian times, a place to which tourists came in good numbers, and developed a network of paths and flimsy wooden bridges from which to admire the spectacle of Yewdale Beck as it plunged through the gill. High above the gill lies a wide marshy hollow, and above that the steep slopes of Lad Stones and Wetherlam.*

The hamlet of Low Tilberthwaite is little more than a row of cottages and a few farms, but it lies in one of the most beautiful nooks of Lakeland, sequestered amid enfolding fells and shielded from view, a place of wild beauty. Once you leave the A593, *great care is needed along the narrow road that leads to Tilberthwaite, which has few passing places.*

From the parking area turn left and walk towards the row of cottages, there leaving the road to walk in front of them, and then through a gate onto a broad stony track that sets off uphill into the embrace of the Tilberthwaite Fells. Almost immediately, leave the track for a branching route on the left, an ascending miners' track that rises across the slopes of Blake Rigg and then changes direction to run on high above the ravine of Tilberthwaite Gill.

The on-going track, stony and rough but otherwise a delight to follow skims around the marshy ground of Dry Cove Ⓐ,

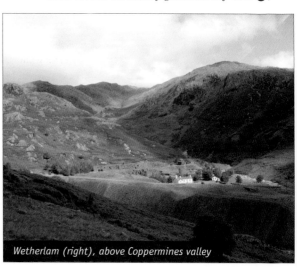

*Wetherlam (right), above Coppermines valley*

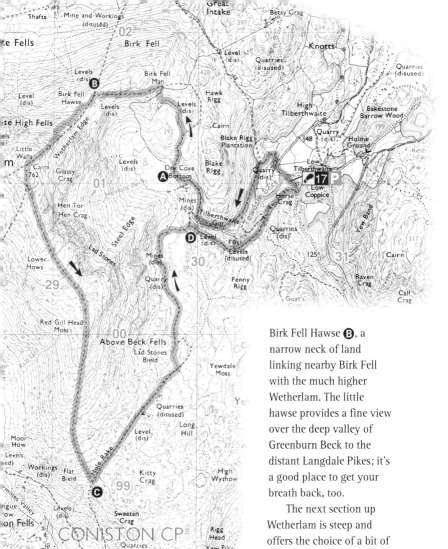

Birk Fell Hawse **B**, a narrow neck of land linking nearby Birk Fell with the much higher Wetherlam. The little hawse provides a fine view over the deep valley of Greenburn Beck to the distant Langdale Pikes; it's a good place to get your breath back, too.

The next section up Wetherlam is steep and offers the choice of a bit of scrambling on a rocky ridge, or something rather easier by way of one of a network of ascending paths, all of which take you ever higher. The summit of Wetherlam is a wide rocky platform with superb views, reaching as far as Ingleborough in the Yorkshire Dales. Much nearer lie Swirl How and the Old Man of Coniston.

The continuation sets off in a southerly direction, towards a conspicuous cairn, following an improving path that cavorts around and over rocky knolls and tarn-filled hollows, eventually heading south-east

rarely dry, and once flooded to provide power for a waterwheel at Tilberthwaite mine. That this area was extensively mined is obvious enough, but the layout of the ruins, first of Hellen's Mine, and later those of Borlase Mine, takes a while to figure out. The track, however, is quite clear, climbing steadily, and, for a while, more steeply as it heads for

Tilberthwaite quarry

to skitter down to a path near the top of Hole Rake Pass **C**.

Go left on a good path, passing a small tarn from which you accompany Crook Beck for a while, but skirting some of the wettest ground before swinging eastwards towards the top of Tilberthwaite Gill. Before long you cross Crook Beck **D** and can follow a path on the south side of the gill. This leads down the opposite side of the ravine used earlier in the walk, and takes you past the Penny Rigg quarry, the entrance to which lies through a tall but narrow gap in the rocks. *Take care because once inside the quarry there are a number of unfenced drops: children and dogs need to be suitably tethered.*

### Tilberthwaite Quarries

Slate quarrying was a mainstay of the Lakeland economy for many years, though inland quarries, like Penny Rigg, had only a limited period of prosperity supplying a mainly local market. Enterprising merchants, like Thomas Rigge of Hawkshead, was exporting the lovely Tilberthwaite green slate as long ago as 1818, contriving, long before the railway came to Coniston, to transport it via Coniston Water to Greenodd, from where it went by sloop to seaports across England and Ireland.

Beyond the quarry, the path descends steadily and soon meets the roadside parking at the start of the walk.

**18** *Great Dodd and Clough Head*

8 miles (13km)

1,970 feet (600m)

**19** *Sheffield Pike*

5 miles (8km)

1,790 feet (545m)

**20** *Helvellyn via Striding Edge and Grisedale*

10¾ miles (17.3km)

3,605 feet (1,100m)

**21** *Fairfield*

10½ miles (17km)

3,525 feet (1,075m)

**22** *St Sunday Crag*

8¾ miles (14km)

2,755 feet (840m)

**23** *Yoke, Ill Bell, Froswick and Thornthwaite Crag*

11¼ miles (18.2km)

3,150 feet (960m)

**24** *High Street and Harter Fell*

7 miles (11km)

2,675 feet (815m)

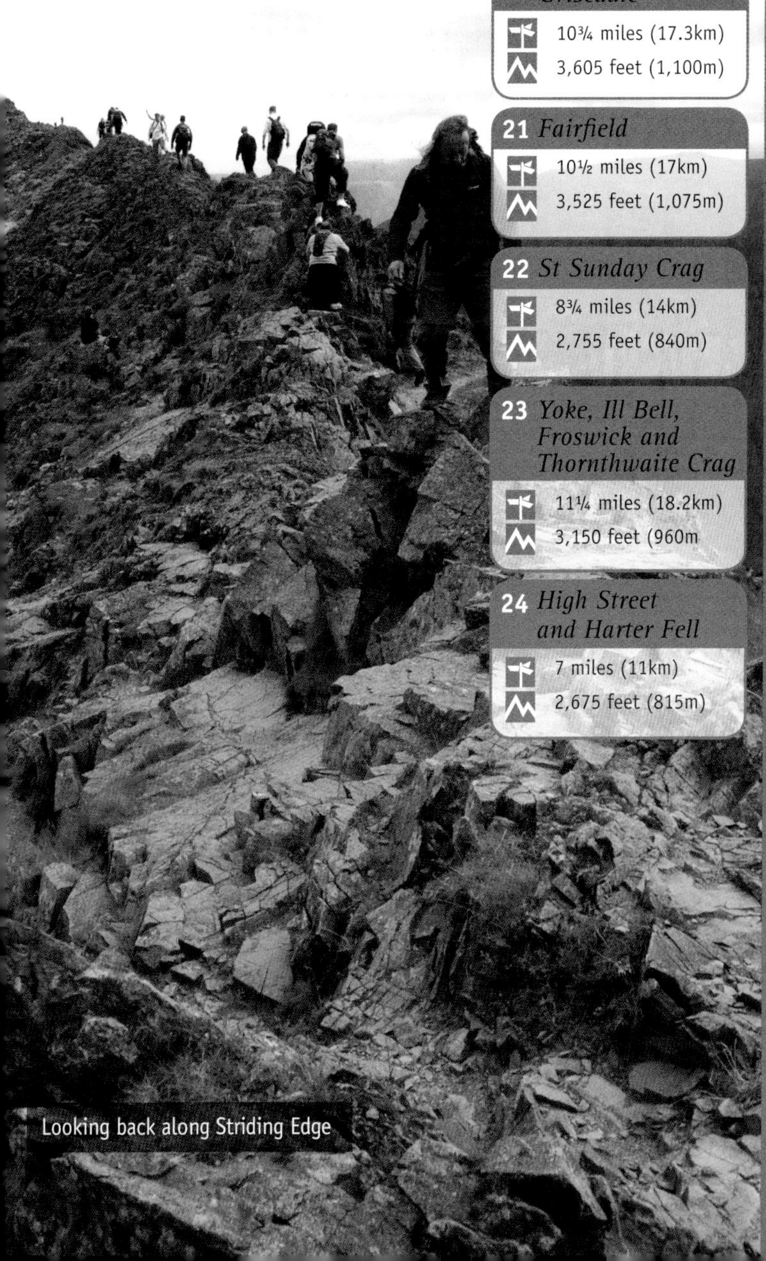

Looking back along Striding Edge

# Eastern Lakeland

*The summit of Sheffield Pike*

Everything that lies to the east of the central divide that runs from Windermere to Keswick falls to be described as 'Eastern' Lakeland, although there are degrees of eastern-ness. As you travel from Ambleside northwards to Thirlmere and St John's in the Vale, so your right-hand view is blocked by the seemingly endless bulk of mountains from Fairfield to Helvellyn and the long, curvy uplands of the Dodds. Proximity to civilisation and ease of access make these fells popular, whether from the west or the long valley of Patterdale.

But east of Patterdale the fells roll on across Place Fell and High Street to distant Haweswater-filled Mardale and summits that are less well-known, but which have a place on the stage of the Lakeland fell drama as worthy as any other member of the cast.

There is cragginess here, narrow ridges, soaring heights, lakes and tarns by the score and myriad ways ancient and modern across the fells. And, if such is your wont, an isolation and remoteness that will gladden your heart.

Here beside the waters of Patterdale's lake, Dorothy Wordsworth noticed the daffodils that later inspired her brother; and onto the lake the earliest visitors came to hear cannons fired and French horns played so that they might experience the echoes. These eastern fells, awkward of access, drew the Victorian crowds, and offered, then as now, an escapism and enjoyment that is unrivalled.

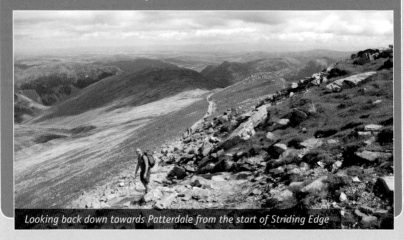
*Looking back down towards Patterdale from the start of Striding Edge*

# Great Dodd and Clough Head

*There is a cleanness of line about the Dodds that ought to attract legions of fell wanderers. And yet it is that very simplicity that seems to propel walkers elsewhere in search of rugged crags, deep valleys and raging torrents. But here it is all grass, reeds and expansive, curvaceous moorland that goes by the name Matterdale Common. As with Gowbarrow Park, not so far distant and where Dorothy Wordsworth noticed the daffodils about which her brother penned his most popular poem, up here among the Dodds you really can wander lonely as a cloud.*

## walk 18

**Start**
High Row

**Distance**
8 miles (13km)

**Height gain**
1,970 feet (600m)

**Route terrain**
Mainly rough moorland

**Parking**
Very limited parking at High Row

**OS maps**
Explorer OL5 (English Lakes – North-eastern area)

**GPS waypoints**
NY 380 219
Ⓐ NY 373 221
Ⓑ NY 348 210
Ⓒ NY 337 228
Ⓓ NY 350 227

There is very limited parking at High Row, so you may have to add some distance to the day by starting at the car park at NY 397 211 along the A5091, and following the road to Dockray and then High Row from there.

It is at High Row that you can access the Old Coach Road that curls round the northern end of the Dodds to St John's in the Vale. Follow this ancient highway until you reach the footbridge/ford at Groove Beck Ⓐ. Leave the old road here to gain a path past a sheepfold and out onto the vastness of Matterdale Common. If you achieve a completely dry-shod ascent, then you have had a lucky day, but only after prolonged rain is the going arduous. Otherwise, just keep plodding

*Bracken fronds in autumn*

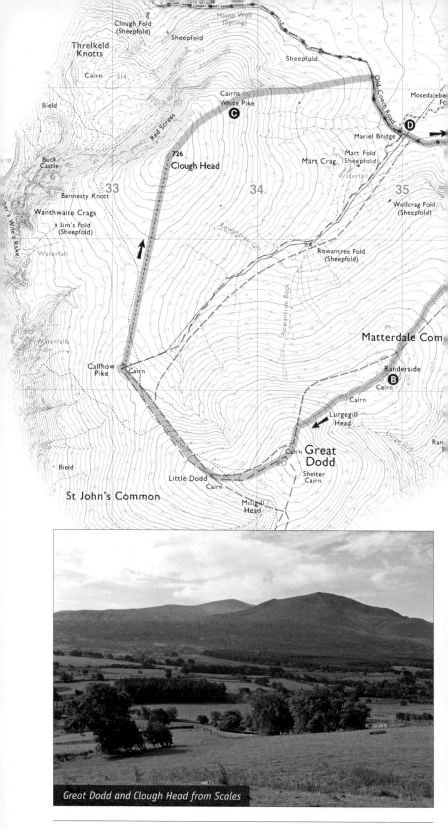

Great Dodd and Clough Head from Scales

Whitesike Moss
Bield (dis)
Caral Beck
Thornsgill Beck
376
New Road
392
Ba
Barbaryrigg Moss
Sandbeds Moss
Barbaryrigg Fold
Barbary Rigg
Wolfcrag Moss
her Sike
White Sike
Hazelhow End
455
Cockley Moor
440
36
37
38
420
541
Ford
**A**
Groovebeck Fold
FB
Red Moss
**18**
390
412
Sheepfold
High Row
Bank
Lucy's Wood
Whams Moss
Little Pike
Cuddy Crag
Horsemire Head
Groove Beck
Blake Sike
Beckbottom
Low How
497
Crookwath
FB
ss
High Brow 575
480
FB
Ford
Dowthwaitehead Moss
Dowthwaite Crag
Rush Gill
Weir

0   200   400   600   800 METRES   1
KILOMETRES
MILES
0   200   400   600 YARDS   ½

SCALE 1:25000 or 2½ INCHES to 1 MILE 4CM to 1KM

onwards and upwards to the cairned prominence of Randerside **B**. From there it is a brief, easy pull onto the summit of Great Dodd, adorned by a low cairn and a shelter some distance away.

The continuation to Clough Head is initially westwards, descending easily to Little Dodd before curving to the north-west to reach the knobbly little upthrust of Calfhow Pike, from where it is a straight-forward romp, gently uphill to the trig pillar on Clough Head, a fine viewpoint for the ribbed profile of Blencathra.

*In poor visibility, it is important to remember that Clough Head has steep drops, scree and crags to the north and west, and that the only safe way down lies between north-east and south-east.* This is rough, largely untracked moorland, and you can choose your own line. But on a clear day, head first for White Pike **C**, which is a delightful

place to relax before quitting the fells altogether. There is a fine view over Matterdale from here to the low mounds of Great and Little Mell Fell.

The Old Coach Road below, essentially a rough track bounded by a fence, crosses Moredale Beck at Mariel Bridge, your next objective. There is no path and no particular line so, it really is a question of choosing a way down that you are comfortable with, and then taking the descent steadily. Keeping away from Mosedale Beck feeder streams will help to speed progress.

Once on the Old Coach Road again, turn right to Mariel Bridge **D**, and then simply stride out along the road back to High Row. Bear in mind, however, that the Coast-to-Coast Cycle Route passes along the Old Coach Road, which you will have to share with cyclists. ●

# Sheffield Pike

**Start**
Glenridding

**Distance**
5 miles (8km)

**Height gain**
1,790 feet (545m)

**Route terrain**
Mine tracks, rough fell walking, craggy outcrops, steep descent

**Parking**
Glenridding (Pay and Display)

**OS maps**
Explorer OL5 (English Lakes – North-eastern area)

**GPS waypoints**
NY 386 169
Ⓐ NY 379 169
Ⓑ NY 362 182
Ⓒ NY 373 178
Ⓓ NY 378 175

*Glenridding has long been a tourist hotspot. In the 18th century visitors would be rowed out into the lake while cannons were fired or musicians played French horns, so that the tourists could listen to the echoes. At the time, this popular 'tourist' destination was also a major mining area. The mining evidence is still there, but it is tucked conveniently out of sight at the top end of Glenridding. Taking the opportunity to visit the mining area, this walk then climbs onto Sheffield Pike, a fell that dominates the north side of Glenridding but which sees far fewer walkers than others in this area.*

Leave the car park by walking out to the road and turning right to cross Glenridding Bridge. Immediately turn right onto a narrow lane for 'Miresbeck' and 'Helvellyn'. Pass a whitewashed cottage with circular chimneys typical of Lakeland's vernacular architecture, probably dating from the late 18th century. Beyond this the lane becomes a stony track. When it forks, branch right and go towards Glenridding Beck, now following a lovely track around a camp site to emerge onto a surfaced lane at Gillside.

Turn right and cross Rattlebeck Bridge Ⓐ. The on-going lane comes out at a wider road. Go left, climbing gently and when, shortly, it forks, keep left again for 'Greenside Mine' and 'Sticks Pass', to pass below rows of terraced cottages that once served the miners and their families.

The fells on your right (north) are Glenridding Dodd and Sheffield Pike, while to the south looms the massive bulk of Birkhouse Moor. The on-going track is most satisfying and ambles easily up towards the mining site.

*Sheffield Pike and Heron Pike from Glenridding*

> **Greenside lead mine** Lead ore was first discovered at Greenside in the 1650s, the first levels being driven by Dutch adventurers in the 1690s, and dressed ore was carried to the smelter at Keswick. Production at the mine, however, did not really begin until the late 18th century, and the mine was not extensively worked until 1825. Mining activity reached maximum production after the Greenside Mining Company was set up in 1822. At the height of its activity, the mine was not only the largest lead mine in the Lake District, with over 300 employees, but was also a pioneer, being the first to use electricity to power the winding gear, and the first underground electric engine in British ore mines.
>
> Power was originally provided by waterwheels, the water being supplied by the damming of nearby tarns. One of them, Keppel Cove, burst its banks on 29 October 1927, bringing disaster to the village below. Much the same happened four years later, when flood waters smashed through the concrete of High Dam.
>
> By the early 1960s, the mine had become uneconomic, and it closed, the last ore being extracted in April 1961. But that was not entirely the end of the story for the mine was then used to test instruments designed to detect underground nuclear explosions. Most of the mine buildings are now gone, but a few remain and see service as a youth hostel and mountain huts; in fact, a bridge seat at Swart Beck is a perfect place to take a breather.

Follow the path as it climbs past the youth hostel, crosses Swart Beck and then by a waymarked route threads a group of buildings to gain a track bound for Red Tarn and Helvellyn. The onward route, however, quickly shuns this track and turns right, signed for

SCALE 1:25000 or 2½ INCHES to 1 MILE 4CM to 1KM

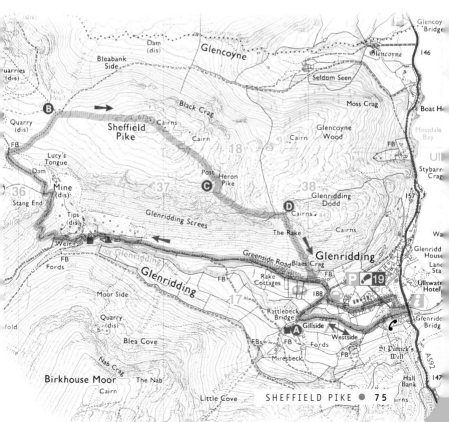

'Sticks Pass', climbing in zigzags up the steep slope above until, as the gradient eases, you reach a stone footbridge taking you back across Swart Beck. Now a steady pull takes you up to Nick Head **B**, a linking, grassy col between Sheffield Pike and Stybarrow Dodd.

As you approach Nick Head, bear right onto a peaty path that climbs to the top of Sheffield Pike, which is crowned by a fine cairn. This is a satisfying place and one you may have to yourself (or not). But there is plenty of room to settle down for a breather, while you take in the views.

The continuation from Sheffield Pike summit needs a little care to begin with, to ensure that you locate the correct path, first to Heron Pike, which is in view from the top of Sheffield Pike, and then onwards and downwards. The main direction is south-east, and a clear and continuous path takes you first to Heron Pike **C**, from where you need to look to the southern side of the fell to locate another narrow path, tortuous and twisting in extravagant style as it guides you down to a wall gap just above the col **D**, Rake Head, linking to Glenridding Dodd.

Clear paths run left, right and ahead onto Glenridding Dodd (which is an optional extra, from which you need to return to the col **D**). From the col, head east-of-south towards Glenridding, descending steeply down the southern flank of Glenridding Dodd until you reach the mine track used earlier in the walk. *You can now simply retrace your steps, or (shorter) turn right towards Glenridding Beck but then immediately turn left to walk down along a row of old cottages to return to the Glenridding car park.* ●

*The summit of Sheffield Pike*

# Helvellyn via Striding Edge and Grisedale

## walk 20

**Start**
Patterdale

**Distance**
10¾ miles (17.3km)

**Height gain**
3,605 feet (1,100m)

**Route terrain**
*A high mountain undertaking requiring scrambling ability. Some exposure on Striding Edge (mostly avoidable). A good head for heights would be useful*

**Parking**
Opposite Patterdale Hotel (Pay and Display)

**OS maps**
Explorer OL5 (English Lakes – North-eastern area)

**GPS waypoints**
⌖ NY 396 159
Ⓐ NY 383 156
Ⓑ NY 359 155
Ⓒ NY 342 144
Ⓓ NY 357 137
Ⓔ NY 389 159

*At once both inspirational and awe-inspiring, the traverse of Striding Edge may well be the most popular high-level outing in the Lake District. The route is the stuff of dreams, drawing every fell-walking ambition sooner or later, and frustrating a few. Technically, the walking is not difficult, but the sense of exposure is in places a little intimidating (although almost all can be avoided). But before setting foot on Helvellyn itself, there is a brief downwards scramble at the end of Striding Edge that often causes a people jam as you wait for others to figure it out. From the summit, the walk heads south along a fine high level route to Dollywaggon Pike, finishing down delightful Grisedale.*

⌖ Turn left out of the car park and, opposite the **White Lion**, go right onto a path climbing past public toilets. At the rear of an isolated building leave the track by turning left onto a path through bracken and heather. This leads to a gate giving onto open fellside, from where a path climbs rockily for a short while before descending to a kissing-gate to the left of two other gates. Through this, follow the adjacent wall, then climb to a level path before descending gently to cross Hag Beck on stepping stones. The path continues easily, crossing the slopes of Glenamara Park and the much steeper slopes below Thornhow End.

Stay along the path, beside a wall above a pine plantation, and then maintain a level course when the wall drops away to the right. A short way on, the path rejoins a wall and leads to a gate. Through the gate, continue descending beside a wall to a couple of sheepfolds. There turn right through a gate, going down field, past a barn to a surfaced track. Turn right to a gate Ⓐ, and immediately go left, soon crossing Grisedale Beck. Stay with the lane for a short distance farther, until, at a bend, you can leave it, through a small gate, to ascend a steep pasture to another gate and wall.

Beyond the gate, the path goes left and immediately forks. The lower branch sets off into Grisedale, while the higher, the route to be taken, begins the long and gradually rising

approach to Striding Edge. As you climb, the view of Grisedale below becomes more and more impressive, brought abruptly to a halt by the crags of Nethermost Pike and Dollywaggon

Pike at the head of the dale.

After a steady climb of about 1¼ miles, the path spreads in a broad spill of loose stones that heralds the so-called Hole in the Wall **B**, a wall

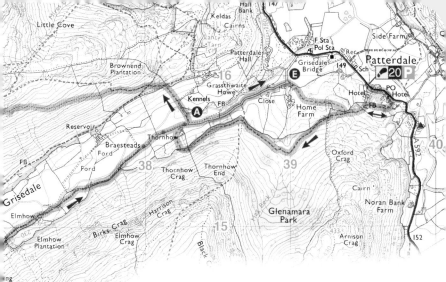

gap denoting
the start of
Striding Edge.
Beyond the gap, a few
scattered rocks overlooking
Grisedale offer an opportunity
to take a break. It is here that
Helvellyn and its neighbour Catstye
Cam first come into view, above the
hollow that houses Red Tarn.

Striding Edge ripples along the left-
hand edge of the hollow, and you follow
an easy path heading towards it. Those
having no problem with heights and the
ability to scramble a little, should
consider leaving the main path, to
follow the crest of the approaching
ridge; it gives splendid views of
Grisedale and St Sunday Crag.
Eventually, both this approach and the
path join at the start of the Edge proper.
*From this point, anyone who is
uncomfortable in exposed situations
should locate a path, low down on the
Red Tarn side, by means of which you
can circumvent all the difficulties of the
Edge.* The rest begin by working a way
round the right edge of the rocky
buttress immediately ahead, beyond
which a number of precarious paths
weave along Striding Edge.

Towards the end of the Edge, the path
directs you, rather awkwardly for a
stride or two, to the top of a short
descending gully. This is most easily
descended by facing inwards; there are
plenty of good hand and foot holds,
and the difficulties are more imagined
than real.

Once beyond this brief scramble, all
that remains is the bulging shoulder of
Helvellyn. A little more, easy scrambling
awaits as the on-going route climbs to
the edge of the summit plateau. A
nearby memorial, overlooking Red
Tarn, commemorates Charles Gough
of Manchester, and his faithful dog.

The summit of Helvellyn may come
as something of an anticlimax; a broad,
largely featureless plateau. A cross-
shelter provides refuge from most winds,
and beyond it a short step up leads to
the highest point, marked by a lonely
trig point.

From the summit, about face, heading
to the right of the shelter and soon
passing a low memorial to John Leeming
and Bert Hinkler who landed a light
aircraft here in 1926. Now follow a
broad and clear path that descends to
a col **C** just north of Nethermost Pike.

*Striding Edge from Nethermost Pike*

Here, the path divides, the right-hand branch descending to Wythburn. But you should keep left, climbing onto Nethermost Pike to enjoy an elevated trek across stony ground towards Dollywaggon Pike. You will need to deviate from the path to 'bag' both Nethermost Pike and Dollywaggon Pike, although the path is a sure option in poor visibility.

### Brothers' Parting Stone

Barely legible, a memorial placed by Canon Rawnsley on a boulder just below the path marks the spot where, on 29 September 1800, William Wordsworth last saw his brother John in the Lake District, who died on 5 February 1805 when his ship sank off Portland Bill. William and Dorothy met John on a few occasions subsequently in London, giving the lie to the popular notion that they last met here at Grisedale Tarn.

Once beyond Dollywaggon Pike, descend steeply to the bowl containing Grisedale Tarn, gradually swinging left (eastwards) to follow a path down into the head of Grisedale.

Following the path down into Grisedale, flanked as it is to the south by the steep slopes first of Fairfield, and then of St Sunday Crag, you soon arrive at an isolated building, Ruthwaite Lodge, a climbing hut. Below the lodge, the path soon divides **D**, and you can go either way, although the preferred way is to the right. This leads steadily down, bounding around through glacial moraine, but finally becoming a broad track and then a surfaced farm access, which leads to the junction **A**, encountered earlier in the walk. Go forward through the field gate and down the road until it makes a pronounced left turn. Here leave it by branching right onto a wide track **E**. Shortly, leave the track at a waymark, pass through a kissing-gate, and follow a waymarked route across rough pasture to a high through-stile in a wall. Over the wall, rejoin the outward route. Turn left to follow it back to the start. ●

# Fairfield

*The circuit of the Rydal Beck watershed from Ambleside is one of the classic routes in Lakeland, and deservedly so. But, better known as the Fairfield Horseshoe, it is no light undertaking, and the plateau-like summit of Fairfield is confusing in misty conditions. The great bulk of Fairfield comes into view once the eastern ridge is gained at Low Pike, and continues to draw you on until finally you make it. The whole circuit, one that hardy fell-runners complete each May in around 90 minutes, is for most folk a full day of energetic exercise.*

## walk

**Start**
Ambleside

**Distance**
10½ miles (17km)

**Height gain**
3,525 feet (1,075m)

**Route terrain**
Rough fell walking, craggy outcrops

**Parking**
There is plenty of parking in Ambleside (Pay and Display)

**OS maps**
Explorers OL5 (English Lakes – North-eastern area) and OL7 (English Lakes – South-eastern area)

**GPS waypoints**
- NY 377 045
- **A** NY 376 066
- **B** NY 374 104
- **C** NY 356 104
- **D** NY 356 083

The key to the start is Nook Lane, reached from the Market Cross in Ambleside by walking up North Road, past the ancient **Unicorn Inn** to the junction with Kirkstone Road. Here, turn left and descend Smithy Brow past the **Golden Rule Inn**, then take the next turning on the right, crossing the end of Tom Fold, and entering Nook Lane. *Walkers starting from the large car park along the main road, north of the centre, can gain the foot of Smithy Brow more easily, turning up this, and then left into Nook Lane.*

The lane rises pleasantly past the University of Cumbria to reach Nook End Farm. Keep forward and go through a gate, then take the left-hand, descending path that leads down to Low Sweden Bridge, where Scandale Beck bubbles through a wooded ravine. The broad path on the other side curves up into and through sloping pastures, bringing views of the distant Langdale Pikes, Bow Fell, Crinkle Crags and the Coniston Fells.

There is a clear track up through the pastures, which, higher up, are dense with bracken. This is agreeable walking, rising steadily all the while with forward views mainly over Scandale on the right. The path divides at a low waymark **A**, now with Brock Crags in view, over-topped by High Pike beyond.

The path branches left, keeps below Brock Crags and finally swings round them to approach a substantial wall rising along the ridge to Low Pike and High Pike, a marvellous piece of craftsmanship that has endured for hundreds of years. The easiest way to 'bag' Low Pike is to stay with the path, passing below Low Pike and rising to meet the wall, and then simply backtrack beside the wall to this minor first summit of the round. It is a splendid viewpoint.

Now press on beside the wall, soon crossing a ladder-stile and engaging ever-rising ground and rock steps to reach the top of High Pike. Anyone expecting more rock work is in for a disappointment; the top of High Pike is a sloping plateau of grass with little rock other than that on which a cairn is perched.

Dove Crag lies ahead, up a long grassy slope, which you tread still in company with the wall. But as Dove Crag is approached the wall finally crumbles into little-or-nothingness, a humble shadow of its former self.

First impressions suggest that Dove Crag **B** has little to detain you. But if you continue north to a small cairn amid a rash of stones, a stunning view opens up of Helvellyn, St Sunday Crag, Place Fell and the far eastern fells. Out of sight below your feet, the cliffs of Dove Crag pose classic routes for rock gymnasts.

As the route presses on, still escorted

### Rydal Mount

Rydal Mount was the home of William Wordsworth in his final years, from 1813 until his death in 1850. The house enjoys glorious views of Windermere, Rydal Water and the surrounding fells. It now belongs to descendants of the poet, and retains a lived-in family atmosphere, having changed little since Wordsworth came here. They rented the house from Lady le Fleming, of nearby Rydal Hall. The house contains portraits, personal possessions and first editions of the poet's work. Wordsworth was a keen gardener, and the large garden remains much as he designed it. After his daughter Dora died in 1847, Wordsworth went down to a small field behind the church, and together with his wife, sister and a gardener, planted hundreds of daffodils as a memorial to Dora. Dora's Field now belongs to the National Trust.

Low Pike

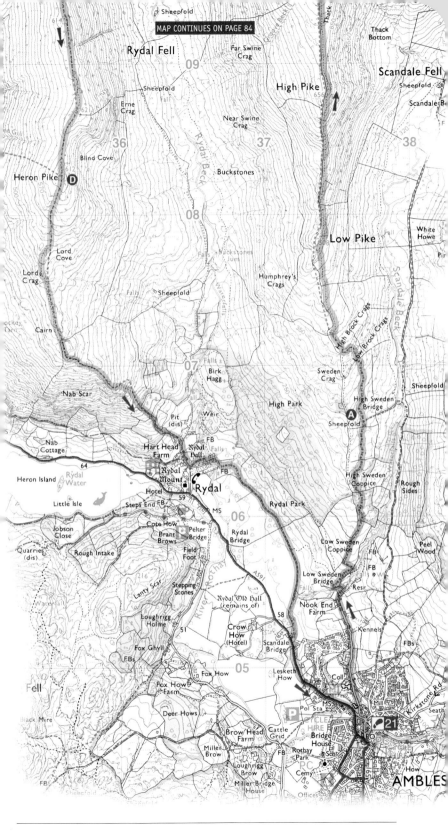

MAP CONTINUES ON PAGE 84

Rydal Fell

Far Swine Crag

High Pike

Scandale Fell

09

Sheepfold

Sheepfold

Scandale B

Erne Crag

Near Swine Crag

36

37

38

Blind Cove

Heron Pike D

Low Pike

White Howe

08

Lord Cove

Buckstones Jum

Lord Crag

Humphrey's Crags

Falls

Sheepfold

ckey Tarn

Cairn

High Brock Crags

Low Brock Crags

Scandale Beck

07

Falls

Birk Hagg

Sweden Crag

Sheepfold

Nab Scar

Falls

High Park

High Sweden Bridge

Pit (dis)

Weir

A

Sheepfold

Nab Cottage

FB

Hart Head Farm

Rydal Hall

High Sweden Coppice

Rough Sides

64

Rydal Mount

FB

Heron Island

Rydal Water

Hotel

Rydal

Little Isle

Steps End FB

59

MS

Rydal Park

Low Sweden Coppice

FB

Peel Wood

Jobson Close

Cote How

Pelter Bridge

06

Rydal Bridge

FB

Quarries (dis)

Brant Brows

Field Foot

Low Sweden Bridge

Resr

Rough Intake

Lanty Scar

216

Stepping Stones

River Rothay

Nook End Farm

FBs

Loughrigg Holme

51

Rydal Old Hall (remains of)

58

Kennels

Fox Ghyll

A591

Crow How (Hotel)

Scandale Bridge

Coll

Kirkstone Rd

FBs

Fell

Fox How

05

Lesketh How

Mill

Seath

Black Mire

Fox How Farm

P

Pol Sta

MS

21

Deer Hows

CLE HIRE

Brow Head Farm

Cattle Grid

Bridge House

Sch

How

Miller Brow

Rothay Park

FB

PC

Loughrigg Brow

Cemy

Liby

AMBLES

FB

Miller Bridge House

Offices

Sheepfold

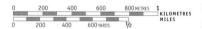

The map contains the following labels:

Stepping Stones · Cawk Cove · (The Forces Waterfalls) · Fall · Cofa Pike · Black Buttress · Hutaple Crag · Greenhow End · Erne Nest Crag · **12** · Hog Hole · The Step · Black Tippet · Blake Brow · Cairn · Flinty Grave · Link Cove · **Fairfield** · Mounds · Pile of Stones · Cairn · Scrubby Crag · Hause Gap Cairn · Fairfield Brow · Hause Moss · Rain Gauge · Link Hause · Shelter · **Hart Crag** · Houndshope Cove · **Rydal Head** · Cairns · Nettle Cove · Black Crag · **11** · Priest's Hole (Cave) · Waterfall · Calf Cove · Dove Crag · **B** · **35** · **Great Rigg** · **C** · **36** · **37** · Greatrigg Man (Cairn) · Cairn · Stone Cove · **10** · Dalehead Close · Cai · Scandale · Waterfall · Thack Bottom Edge · Gooere Beck · Sheepfold · Rydal Fell · Far Swine Crag · Thac Bottc · **09** · Greenhead Gill · S

by a now seriously dilapidated wall, the going becomes more rocky. *First you tackle the rocks of Hart Crag and then another rocky rise to gain the summit of Fairfield, a vast, largely featureless plateau on which skilled navigation is vital in poor visibility.* This popular summit, however, seems to hold little of interest, but to the north lie ice-fashioned corries and shapely ridges leading onwards to distant Helvellyn and round eastwards to St Sunday Crag that do much to redeem Fairfield's character.

Now the descent, which sets off briefly east of south, and then west of south down an increasing slope that leads down to Great Rigg **C**, before enjoying a fine romp over the bumps of Rydal Fell and Heron Pike. As you leave Heron Pike **D** you begin the long, rocky descent of Nab Scar, which in recent years has seen much path-improvement work. Eventually, the descending path emerges at a lane head, close by Rydal Mount.

At the top of the lane, a track bears off past Rydal Hall, soon crossing Rydal Beck and then following a route across Rydal Park to emerge on the Ambleside road at Scandale Bridge. Now simply follow the main road to get back into Ambleside. ●

Scale bar:
0 — 200 — 400 — 600 — 800 METRES — 1 KILOMETRES / MILES
0 — 200 — 400 — 600 YARDS — ½

SCALE 1:25000 or 2½ INCHES to 1 MILE 6CM to 1KM

# St Sunday Crag

**Start**
Patterdale

**Distance**
8¾ miles (14km)

**Height gain**
2,755 feet (840m)

**Route terrain**
Rough tracks and fell
walking, craggy
outcrops, steep
descent

**Parking**
Opposite Patterdale
Hotel (Pay and
Display)

**OS maps**
Explorer OL5 (English
Lakes – North-eastern
area)

**GPS waypoints**
NY 396 159
**A** NY 382 156
**B** NY 355 135
**C** NY 351 122
**D** NY 361 126

*Grisedale is a gloriously rugged dale, farmed in the valley
bottom and networked by striking drystone walls. This is a gem
and well worth wandering up and down at any time of the year.
Here, it is used as a lengthy, roundabout route to the summit of
St Sunday Crag, which bounds it on the south, spewing rock
and scree down impossible slopes.*

Most ascents of St Sunday Crag from Patterdale start the
climb via Thornhow End, but this is unremittingly steep all the
way to the summit, and while the present alternative involves
exactly the same amount of height gain, it all comes in fairly
easy stages, rather than abruptly.

Leave the car park, and turn left to cross the road.
Opposite the **White Lion Hotel**, turn right onto a path climbing
past toilets. Soon, at the rear of an isolated building, leave the
track by turning left onto a path through bracken and heather
that leads to a gate giving onto open fellside, with an already
impressive forward view of St Sunday Crag's formidable
northern slopes rising steeply above Glenamara Park.

The path climbs through rocks and small boulders for a short
while before descending to a kissing-gate to the left of two
other gates. Through this, follow the continuing wall, then
climb to a horizontal path before descending gently to cross
Hag Beck on stepping stones. The path runs on easily across
Glenamara Park and the steeper slopes below Thornhow End.

Follow the path as it leads alongside a wall bounding a pine
plantation, and then maintain a level course as the wall drops
away to the right. A short way on, the path rejoins a wall and
arrives at a gate. Pass through this gate and continue
descending beside a wall to a couple of sheepfolds. There turn
right through another wall gate, going down field, past a barn
to a surfaced track **A**.

Now simply turn left and follow the track up-valley, a simple
task but one that is glorious walking. When the track heads for
Braesteads Farm, keep ahead onto a graded track to Elmhow
Farm. After the farm, the path becomes increasingly rugged as
you penetrate to the heart of the high fells and into a harsher,
upland environment. This is splendid walking, and there is an
intense sense of isolation here as all around fell slopes (and
walls) soar upwards.

Continue climbing with increasing ruggedness underfoot until you cross Grisedale Beck. A rough path now leads on to join a path descending from nearby Ruthwaite Lodge **B**.

Press on beyond the lodge, with the ground ahead now obviously easing. Off to the left a boulder bears a memorial to the Lakeland parting of Wordsworth from his brother John (*see Walk 20*). Keep on up to Grisedale Tarn **C**, which is a celebrated oasis and not in view until the last moment.

Now you must turn your attention to St Sunday Crag. From near the outflow of Grisedale Tarn you need to locate and follow a path rising obliquely across the northern slopes of Cofa Pike to reach Deepdale Hause **D**. Now turn onto a gradually broadening ridge that rises in splendid fashion to the top of St Sunday Crag.

Cross the top of St Sunday Crag to a large cairn, and from there start down the north-east ridge to the col linking with Birks, a grassy interlude from where a clear path continues the descent into Grisedale to rejoin your outward route below Glenamara Park.

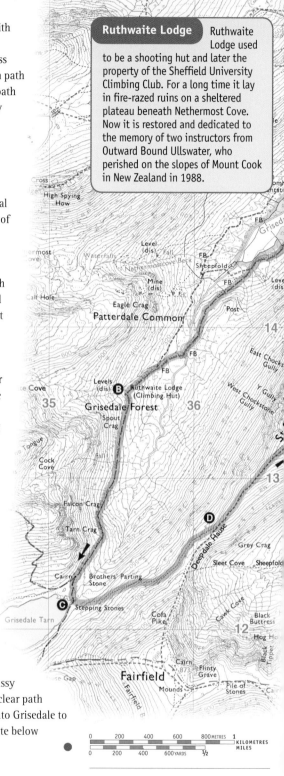

**Ruthwaite Lodge** Ruthwaite Lodge used to be a shooting hut and later the property of the Sheffield University Climbing Club. For a long time it lay in fire-razed ruins on a sheltered plateau beneath Nethermost Cove. Now it is restored and dedicated to the memory of two instructors from Outward Bound Ullswater, who perished on the slopes of Mount Cook in New Zealand in 1988.

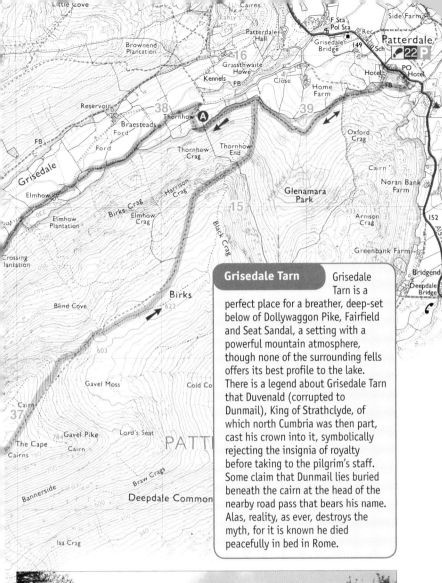

## Grisedale Tarn

Grisedale Tarn is a perfect place for a breather, deep-set below of Dollywaggon Pike, Fairfield and Seat Sandal, a setting with a powerful mountain atmosphere, though none of the surrounding fells offers its best profile to the lake. There is a legend about Grisedale Tarn that Duvenald (corrupted to Dunmail), King of Strathclyde, of which north Cumbria was then part, cast his crown into it, symbolically rejecting the insignia of royalty before taking to the pilgrim's staff. Some claim that Dunmail lies buried beneath the cairn at the head of the nearby road pass that bears his name. Alas, reality, as ever, destroys the myth, for it is known he died peacefully in bed in Rome.

*Birks and St Sunday Crag from Glenamara Park*

**walk 23**

| Start |
| --- |
| Troutbeck |

| Distance |
| --- |
| 11¼ miles (18.2km) |

| Height gain |
| --- |
| 3,150 feet (960m) |

| Route terrain |
| --- |
| Rough fell tracks |

| P Parking |
| --- |
| Church Bridge |

| OS maps |
| --- |
| Explorer OL7 (English Lakes – South-eastern area) |

| GPS waypoints |
| --- |
| NY 412 027 |
| Ⓐ NY 417 027 |
| Ⓑ NY 434 044 |
| Ⓒ NY 433 094 |
| Ⓓ NY 429 081 |
| Ⓔ NY 425 064 |
| Ⓕ NY 421 054 |
| Ⓖ NY 416 039 |

# Yoke, Ill Bell, Froswick and Thornthwaite Crag

*These four summits are usually tackled from Kentmere as part of a horseshoe circuit. Here, however, the opportunity is taken to approach them from the south-west before skittering back down into the lovely Troutbeck valley. Use is made on the descent of the Roman road, known as High Street, an ancient thoroughfare clear in parts, less obvious in others.*

From the parking area, turn right to cross the footbridge beside Church Bridge, and walk alongside the road for about 100 yds. Cross the road and head up the stony track opposite. Follow the track as it climbs steadily upwards, and continues easily, later merging with another coming in from the right. Just after this junction Ⓐ, the track forks. Here, keep right, climbing steadily onto and along Garburn Road, a track that leads up to Garburn Pass. As you climb there are appealing views up the valley of Trout Beck and west to the rugged eastern face of Wansfell and Baystones.

The climb up to Garburn Pass Ⓑ is straightforward, and as you reach the top so a path, paved in recent years, branches off (left/north) from a wall corner to take a line, never far from one of Lakeland's magnificent drystone walls, which accompanies you towards the first fell, Yoke. When the wall changes direction, cross it and climb onto the broad end of Yoke, from where you can scamper up to the summit.

From the top of Yoke, albeit the lowest of the summits visited on this walk, the impression is of mountains stacked on mountains, flowing endlessly away in all directions. This is the sort of panorama that so enthralls visitors to Lakeland, a topographical menu of fell-walking delights.

The next summit along the ridge is Ill Bell, a little higher than Yoke, and a shapely cone that is distinct enough to be recognised from afar. From Yoke a clear path leads above Star Crag and Rainsborrow Cove to Ill Bell. The summit is rough and craggy, dotted with numerous cairns.

Onward the way lies across a steep drop into Over Cove and down to Kentmere Reservoir, to Froswick, again higher than the earlier fells, and a miniature replica of Ill Bell.

Now Thornthwaite Crag awaits, but as you leave Froswick,

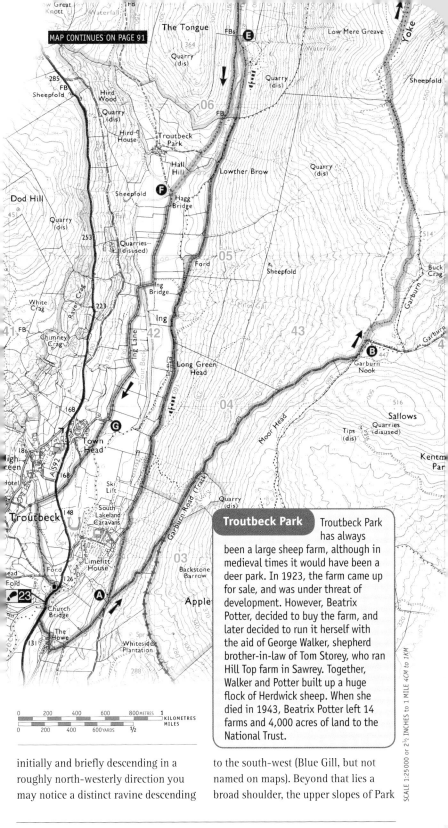

MAP CONTINUES ON PAGE 91

## Troutbeck Park

Troutbeck Park has always been a large sheep farm, although in medieval times it would have been a deer park. In 1923, the farm came up for sale, and was under threat of development. However, Beatrix Potter, decided to buy the farm, and later decided to run it herself with the aid of George Walker, shepherd brother-in-law of Tom Storey, who ran Hill Top farm in Sawrey. Together, Walker and Potter built up a huge flock of Herdwick sheep. When she died in 1943, Beatrix Potter left 14 farms and 4,000 acres of land to the National Trust.

SCALE 1:25000 or 2½ INCHES to 1 MILE 4CM to 1KM

initially and briefly descending in a roughly north-westerly direction you may notice a distinct ravine descending

to the south-west (Blue Gill, but not named on maps). Beyond that lies a broad shoulder, the upper slopes of Park

Fell, and this is the way of your descent. There is a path all the way across Park Fell, known as Scot Rake, although not named as such on maps. As a line of ascent from Troutbeck it can be wearisome, but as a descent it is well worth knowing about. As you now plod onwards to Thornthwaite Crag, keep an eye open for Scot Rake arriving on your left **ⓒ**, and commit the spot to memory.

The continuation to Thornthwaite Crag and its massive summit cairn succumbs to a steady plod, continuing along the excellent path you have used so far. But be sure not to divert to the right; here you need to leave the Roman road, which you joined briefly at the top of Scot Rake, and keep left to Thornthwaite Crag.

---

**Scot Rake** Known in the 18th century as Scots' Rake, this ancient route appears as a steep terraced road, running, it has been suggested, down the length of the valley to Allen Knott, where it would join the Roman road from Watercrook to Ambleside. W G Collingwood suggests that the rake may have been used by Scottish raiders; if so, they were terrible navigators and even worse forward planners, as the confines of Hagg Gill were ideal for ambushes against marauding forces.

The Troutbeck length certainly has a directness about it, and there is a temptation to look on it as Roman in origin. Academics have yet to confirm this pedigree; others suggest it may have been used by peat carriers bound for Windermere.

---

Of three possible ways back to the start, that using Scot Rake is the most direct. You need to retreat the way you came until you locate the top of Scot Rake, then bearing off to your right (south-west) to descend across initially grassy slopes, later turning to bracken as you head for a wall corner **ⓓ** much lower down.

Continue beside the wall for a short distance, and then cross it to gain a pronounced track that parallels Hagg Gill, sandwiched between the ridge you have just walked and another, lower ridge, known as The Tongue. If you want to climb still farther, then once you reach the Hagg Gill track, you can branch right onto the northern end of The Tongue, and follow a grassy, sometimes wet, path all along the highest ground until you are forced steeply downwards to rejoin the Hagg Gill track.

As you stride down the track, you eventually reach a gate **ⓔ**, near a stone barn. *Here you have a choice. If you branch left after the gate and descend to cross Hagg Gill then you join a clear track, probably more of the Roman road, which will guide you unerringly all the way back to the point **ⓐ** where you set off up to Garburn Pass.* The measured route ignores this variation, and continues with the main track, which shortly starts to descend to reach a wall corner. A few strides farther on, leave the track by going left through a kissing-gate onto a path for Troutbeck village. This takes you down across a sloping grassy pasture, keeping to the left of Hall Hill, a large grassy mound.

The descending path reaches the farm access at Hagg Bridge **ⓕ**, and then follows a surfaced lane to Ing Bridge and onward towards Troutbeck village. When the lane turns up towards Town Head, leave it by branching left onto a bridleway **ⓖ** between walls. The bridleway comes out to meet the valley road. Cross, and go into the lane opposite that leads to Troutbeck.

When the lane swings to the right, leave it by branching left onto a path for the church. Confronted by two gates, take that on the right, passing through a kissing-gate to follow the on-going path beside a wall. Shortly the path narrows and runs down between fences. The path is straightforward and leads down to intercept a broad track. Turn left along the side of the graveyard and walk out to the road, there turning right to walk the short distance back to Church Bridge to complete the walk. ●

> **Troutbeck church** The origins of Troutbeck's church are lost, but it certainly existed in the 16th century. The present church was dismantled and rebuilt in 1736, allegedly on the site of a 15th-century chapel. Major restoration was carried out by the Victorians in 1861, and much of the church now displays work of the Arts and Crafts Movement, notably that of Edward Burne-Jones and William Morris. Unusually, the church is not dedicated to a saint, but is known simply as Jesus Church.

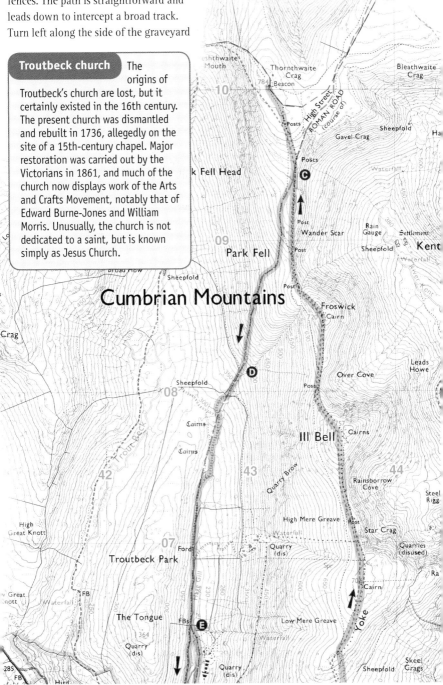

# walk 24

## High Street and Harter Fell

**Start**
Mardale Head
(Haweswater)

**Distance**
7 miles (11km)

**Height gain**
2,675 feet (815m)

**Route terrain**
Rough fell walking,
craggy outcrops

**P Parking**
Mardale road end

**OS maps**
Explorer OL5 (English
Lakes – North-eastern
area)

**GPS waypoints**

NY 469 107
Ⓐ NY 473 114
Ⓑ NY 442 113
Ⓒ NY 452 095
Ⓓ NY 473 093

*Ascents to the flat-topped summit of High Street from the west are preoccupied with others summits. But from the east, at the head of Mardale, there is a fine, undulating rocky ridge, almost arrow-straight that leads directly to the top of High Street. That the ascent can later be combined with that of Harter Fell, the highest summit along the eastern flank of Kentmere, is a bonus.*

The setting at the head of Mardale is wonderful, with high, rocky, steep-sided fells forming the valley headwall, enclosing the southern reaches of this drowned valley. From the car park, pass through the nearby gate, and turn right beside a wall, soon to cross Mardale Beck, and then turn right again, heading for the mature stand of larch and spruce that lays claim to The Rigg, a thumb of rocky ground that sticks out into Haweswater. As you approach the trees, the path starts rising, and finally meets the low end of a ridge at a gap in a wall Ⓐ.

Just before reaching the wall, ascend left, crossing a small hillock draped in bracken, with the formidable profile of Rough Crag looming above you. It seems as impregnable as a medieval fortress, but a path threads a way through or round all obstacles on the way, leaving you free to focus on whether your legs are up to it. Once into your stride, it will be to discover that the going is far less rough than the name suggests, but it remains steep, at least until the summit, marked by a large cairn.

The view from the Rough Crag ridge never fails to make an impression: to the south lies a deep bowl containing Blea Water, overlooked by the slopes of High Street; to the north, Kidsty Pike rises above the wide cove of Riggindale.

Continue along the ridge and descend a little to a grassy col, Caspel Gate, where there is a small pool. Beyond this you

High Street will come as a disappointment if you're expecting shops, cafés and pubs; it's just not that kind of place. The name has its roots in the ancient highway constructed by the Romans across the fell, linking their forts at Ambleside and Penrith. It may seem strange to have constructed a main thoroughfare across high mountains, but 2,000 years ago, the valleys were far less accommodating than they are today; the valley sides were afforested and the valley bottoms were frequently waterlogged and boggy, across which movement would have been slow and tiring. So, the Romans took the high, logical road, across a summit that also came to be known as Racecourse Hill. This was a meeting place for shepherds, who would gather annually to regain sheep that had wandered into another shepherd's domain. Inevitably, such meetings evolved into popular events with races being held across the wide summit of the fell, and fairs being held here until as recently as 1835.

Few these days credit the Romans with originating the 'High Street' road; it seems certain that it was simply an improvement on one known by the 13th century as 'Brettestrete' – the Road of the Britons.

engage an airy, twisting path ascending Long Stile, finally to reach the northern end of High Street **B**. The summit lies a

SCALE 1:25 000 or 2½ INCHES to 1 MILE 4CM to 1KM

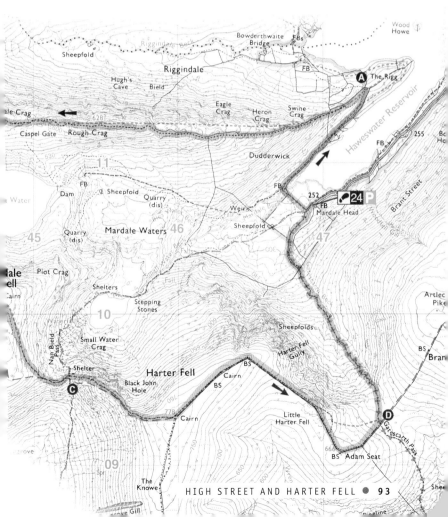

High Street, Rough Crag and Harter Fell (left)

couple of minutes to the south, and the simplest way of finding it in mist is to walk ahead (west) from the top of Long Stile until you intersect a dilapidated wall, and then follow this left (south) to the trig pillar.

From the summit, walk beside the wall to intercept a clear path that crosses a grassy link to Mardale Ill Bell: the right of way shown on the map across High Street is far from distinct on the ground. But, on a clear day, you can more or less head straight for Mardale Ill Bell. This last of the Kentmere west side fells forms a stub of land separating Kentdale and Mardale, and by moving north from the main path for a short distance as you reach the cairned summit, you discover a stunning view of Blea Water lying in its corrie below.

Stay with the path across Mardale Ill Bell, and follow its descent to Nan Bield Pass **C**, an ancient packhorse route crossing point. 'Nant' derives from the Welsh, and means a brook or a gorge, while 'bield' means a sheltered place. A small shelter sits in the middle of the narrow col.

*Walkers wanting to shorten the walk, can dive back to Mardale head from Nan Bield. To do so, turn northwards and begin a stony descent, the path casting about through rocky terrain, eventually to reach a cluster of low stone shelters beside Small Water. Small Water Beck provides some enjoyable cascades as you follow its course towards Haweswater. But steadily the path moves away from the beck as it rounds the northern end of Harter Fell and finally descends to Mardale Head. Taking this option will reduce the overall distance to 5½ miles, and the height gain to 2,130 feet.*

Any steep slope viewed end-on seems steeper than it is; it's a kind of optical illusion. And so it proves with Harter Fell, although the haul upwards is steep enough. But it is short-lived, rising in two steps, and you soon ease onto the almost flat, grassy summit of the fell, marked by a large cairn near a fence.

From here it is virtually all downhill. Turn left beside the fence and pick up a broad path that leads in a north-easterly direction before changing to south-east as it heads for Adam Seat. The descending path by-passes Adam Seat, but it is worth continuing beside the fence to visit this isolated summit, the top of which is marked by a steeple-like marker bearing the letters 'L', for the Lowther Estate, and 'H', possibly for the Howards of Greystoke. From the top of Adam Seat, descend beside the fence to a gate at the top of the Gatescarth Pass **D**.

Now simply turn left and follow the broad stony path down to Mardale Head. ●

Text:                 Terry Marsh
Photography:         Terry Marsh
Editorial:           Ark Creative (UK) Ltd
Design:              Ark Creative (UK) Ltd

This product includes mapping data licensed from Ordnance Survey® with the permission of the Controller of Her Majesty's Stationery Office. © Crown Copyright 2011. All rights reserved. Licence number 150002047. Ordnance Survey, the OS symbol and Pathfinder are registered trademarks and Explorer, Landranger and Outdoor Leisure are trademarks of the Ordnance Survey, the national mapping agency of Great Britain.

ISBN: 978-1-85458-636-0

While every care has been taken to ensure the accuracy of the route directions, the publishers cannot accept responsibility for errors or omissions, or for changes in details given. The countryside is not static: hedges and fences can be removed, stiles become gates, field boundaries can alter, footpaths can be rerouted and changes in ownership can result in the closure or diversion of some concessionary paths. Also, paths that are easy and pleasant for walking in fine conditions may become slippery, muddy and difficult in wet weather, while stepping stones across rivers and streams may become impassable.

If you find an inaccuracy in either the text or maps, please write to Crimson Publishing at the address below.

Printed in Singapore. 1/11

First published in Great Britain 2011 by Crimson Publishing, a division of:
**Crimson Business Ltd,**
Westminster House, Kew Road, Richmond, Surrey, TW9 2ND

www.totalwalking.co.uk

**Front cover:** Robinson from Keskadale
**Page 1:** Looking back down towards Patterdale from the start of Striding Edge

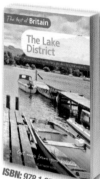